STRUCTURAL
CHANGE AND GROWTH
IN CAPITALISM

STRUCTURAL CHANGE AND GROWTH IN CAPITALISM

A Set of Hypotheses

by PAOLO LEON

translated and revised by the author

The Johns Hopkins Press, Baltimore

PREFACE TO THE AMERICAN EDITION

In this essay, I am trying to establish a series of theses (or, better, hypotheses) in a dynamic setting, predicated on an undemonstrated postulate: that the market system, even in the long run, can survive with its fundamental characteristics unchanged. Although I have tried to give it a reasonable foundation, by introducing the assumption of a special foresight of the entrepreneurial class, I know that I cannot classify that postulate as an economic law. My main attempt, on the other hand, is only a part of the much greater task of understanding how the capitalist system works and the way in which, along with all other historical social forms, it will eventually disappear. The reader, thus, will have to be satisfied with a less than full-fledged analysis.

One is slightly embarrassed when asking for the reader's patience, particularly when fellow economists may be hard put to know why. Most of this essay remains well within established methodology, and one may wonder whether my desire for completeness does not cover a particular ideological bias. My point of departure is that no science can stay put at its experimental stage—particularly in economics, where "experimental" has a confused meaning—and must be able to generate systems of interpretation. On the other hand, it does seem as though economics is losing touch with social reality, paradoxically because of the empirical bias of many economists. Recent empirical research has not really discovered many new economic laws. At the same time, since our science cannot directly experiment and therefore can only test hypotheses on the basis of *ex post facto* data, experiments are always founded on certain reference models. As a result, generalized interpretations are implicit even when experimenting, but little explicit theorizing has gone into them. I am sure I am not alone in thinking that neither Marshall nor Keynes has created—even though each implied—general interpretations, since neither man was able to encompass both thesis and antithesis in his otherwise fruitful theorizing. This line of reasoning becomes particularly confusing when we consider, among the reference models, the neoclassical general equilibrium one: although a general model, it would be extremely difficult to argue that it is a general interpretative scheme. Yet it has gained considerable popularity in the post-war period, particularly in the United States, where it does seem to have been mistaken for an interpretative model; in fact, from it a few economists have drawn the extraordinary conclusion that capitalism is an economic system superior to any other.

This, I thought, was more than enough reason to ask the reader's indulgence in presenting him with another study mostly along traditional lines, even though it does contain an attempt toward a larger vision. I am fully conscious that this attempt cannot be less biased or more objective than the writer's own bias or objectivity. Good and bad ideas do not originate in a political vacuum or by intellectual chance, nor should they be judged on their motivation. In any event, I shall try to leave to the reader, rather than allocating to myself, the task of drawing political conclusions from these pages.

Within the framework of established methodology—that is, without striving for generalized interpretations—some of the hypotheses presented in this essay may have an important practical effect. If such concepts as the differentiation of profit rates, the absence of a production function, and the predominance of the entrepreneurial class are valid, then many economic policies, especially those relating to the long run, must be rethought. In the field of economic policy, the reference schemes mentioned above are used primarily as a justification for choices that have already been made. But when economic policy becomes an instrument in the hands of non-specific interests (such as governments or public enterprises), what was an *ex post facto* justification is very often presented as an *a priori* explanation. And when that justification is wrong or outdated or adapted to the needs of specific interests, economic policies will also be wrong or outdated or adapted to the needs of specific interests. The transformation of reference models into the ideology of economic policy does not happen by chance, as this essay will show, and there may in fact be little that public entities can do independent of or against specific interests. But when the declared public policy objective is to plan for non-specific interests, then it is necessary to realize that those reference models may well be unsuitable. An example will suffice: now that the marginalist theory is dead, investment choices cannot be made on the basis of a general rate of profits (or of interest, or on the basis of an opportunity cost of capital for the economy as a whole) established *ex ante*.

Thus, Harrod-Domar or even Solow-type models are insufficient for economic policies. In this essay I have not been able to consider all the complex questions and problems arising from changing the basic reference model. Also, I have given in these pages only a few possible interpretations. However, if I have succeeded only in offering plausible interpretations or, to be more modest, the basis for future plausible interpretations, I will be satisfied.

As Keynes has written, "the writer . . . treading along unfamiliar paths, is extremely dependent on criticism and conversation if he is to avoid an undue proportion of mistakes. It is astonishing what foolish things one can temporarily believe if one thinks too long alone, particularly in economics. . . ."[1] On the other hand, it is not easy to discuss, outside of an academic environment, themes as complex as those dealt with in this essay. I am particularly grateful, therefore, for the advice and help given me on the occasion of the Italian edition of this book by so many friends, among whom I should like to mention Federico Caffè, Marcello Colitti, Giorgio Fuà, Antonio Giolitti, Mario Marcelletti, Claudio Napoleoni, Romano Pantanali, Gabriele Sciolli, and Luigi Spaventa. I am also very grateful to Vinod Dubey, who has read the English version and made many valuable suggestions. Joyce Buccini has given me invaluable help in correcting, editing, and finally typing the manuscript.

The journals *Studi economici* and *Rivista internazionale di scienze economiche e commerciali* have kindly given permission to utilize parts of articles I published there. Quotations from Joan Robinson's *The Accumulation of Capital* are made by permission of Macmillan & Co. Ltd.

Finally, I want to thank my wife, whose patience and affection have made this book possible.

Washington, D.C.   PAOLO LEON
November, 1966

---

[1] J. M. Keynes, *The General Theory of Employment, Interest and Money* (London, 1936), p. vii.

CONTENTS

INTRODUCTION

In these pages, an attempt is made to offer some basis for a generalized interpretation of the structure and the development process of the capitalist system. The principal elements of this essay are:

1. a distinction between the short and the long run, based on a hypothesis that the subsistence level of consumption is variable;

2. a hypothesis concerning the expectations and the behavior of entrepreneurs, which is not only useful in order to simplify the analysis of the process of formation of long-run decisions, but also reflects an aspect of reality of central importance for the conservation of the capitalist system;

3. a hypothesis which considers the rate of profit not as a uniform rate in the economy as a whole but as a structure of rates originating from the mode of development of consumption; with this hypothesis a definite role will be given to monopolistic market forms, and monopolies thus become a result of the development process; and

4. a wider formulation of the position of predominance of production over consumption, valid over a long period of time.

The hypothesis concerning entrepreneurial behavior and that concerning the predominance of production over consumption will not be readily accepted. The introduction of so-called exogenous factors in order to justify equilibrium of the economic system is always suspected of "sociologism." I believe, instead, that to postulate an economic system (in which *tout se tient*) without taking into account those factors represents an incomplete examination of reality. After all, even though an abstract model and extreme simplifications are used, the task of economists is to attempt to examine the economic system as it manifests itself.

In this essay, random phenomena will acquire considerable importance, especially in the analysis of the technical conditions of production. Following Machiavelli, "Fortune is half the arbiter of every action." In these pages random phenomena are not allowed to determine decisions in the economic field, but they do limit the results of such decisions.

I avoid the use of modern analytical tools[1] (such as input-output analysis or, even more simply, mathematical language) not only because of my limited experience with them, but also because, for the purpose of this essay, the interpretive ability of many such tools is weak. They are necessary for forecasting and for planning but always require general theoretical schemata as their basis. The input-output matrix does not offer to the interpreter of economic growth more than a static reflection, useful but insufficient, of the interdependence of economic phenomena. Like most statistical tools, the matrix gives only *ex post facto* answers. Moreover, it is becoming more and more evident that there has been a certain amount of misuse of the new tools. Recent economic literature shows a tendency to accept without question those instruments and their results, even when their theoretical bases are unsatisfactory.[2]

I found it impossible to use mathematical language in these pages also because I have adopted a concept of equilibrium and a measure of value which are far less exact than the concepts which make up the determined systems of simultaneous equations (general equilibrium systems). On the other hand, I have no doubt that some of the relationships expressed in the following pages can well be subjected to mathematical formulation.

Considering the problem it sets for itself, this essay should be much more ample. Many aspects of the economic system (e.g., money) are not considered here. The reader is not provided with definitions and explanations of every analytical tool used in these pages (which, in any case, do not differ from those usually employed in our science). Moreover, I am aware that the elements of my construction have not all been studied with the same degree of intensity.

This is an essay in pure theory and partakes of the deficiencies of all abstract logical exercises. Some details (such as Engel's law)

---

[1] Activity analysis is excluded from this essay, since we shall examine only superficially the economics of fixed coefficient production.

[2] See R. E. Quandt's review of P. Sraffa's *Production of Commodities by Means of Commodities: Prelude to a Critique of Economic Theory* (Cambridge, 1960) in the *Journal of Political Economy* (October, 1961), for an example of the excessive importance given to modern analytical tools. For a revealing discussion on this subject, see J. Robinson, J. Downie, *et al.,* "The Present Position of Econometrics," in *Journal of the Royal Statistical Society,* Pt. 3 (1960).

are derived from reality, but I have not tried to give the proof of the hypotheses built upon them.

The growth of capitalism described here is an ideal situation, removed from the uncertainties of reality. The development of capitalism is treated as harmonious and continuous; in fact, it occurs in jerky stages, through struggles, wars, and temporary contradictions. Interspersed with periods of rapid growth are periods of stagnation and crisis. Mine is a simplified model, and it is impossible to utilize it to reduce all the peculiarities of capitalist growth to theoretically explainable steps. For example, continuous full employment conditions are assumed, a clearly unrealistic notion which holds only for some capitalist economies at some moments of time. I assume a homogeneous territorial development. This is also an assumption adopted to simplify my task, and its validity is extremely limited.

I have not tried to justify the existence of capitalism, nor to discover its historical limitations. In this first approximation, I have examined only some of its more important logical components. I also refrain from discussing the characteristics of "neocapitalism," a fashionable word today. In a sense, the following analysis is nothing but an interpretation of "neocapitalism," since the distinctive characteristics of the system which is described below are different from those of the classical Marxian description. On the other hand, those distinctive characteristics are not of recent formation but, more or less in embryo, are part of the original patrimony of capitalism. Actually, I do not believe that a new capitalism exists today. The aims, the means, and the behavior of the capitalist class have not changed significantly. There exist new nuances in the adoption of particular tools both because of the effects of the growth of the system—the widening of its material base—and because of the existence of competing economic systems. And it is only to assure its continuity in the face of these new manifestations of older realities that the capitalist class has somewhat refined some of its own tools.

The subject matter is divided into six chapters, a concluding note, and two appendixes. The first chapter places the study within the context of the discussion of the interpretation of the capitalist economy. The second chapter provides a simple model that will be used in the following analysis and proposes the restrictive assumptions that form it. The next four chapters and the concluding notes constitute the main body of the essay and examine some fundamental relationships of the capitalist economic process. The two appendixes illustrate, very superficially, some problems of an open economy and an aspect of the problem of investment criteria in a planned economy, in the light of the analysis of the principal text.

I have not tried to elaborate my conclusions, and the reader will understand why. The structure of capitalism and the laws which its development follows are too complex to furnish simple conclusions: these rest in the description and in the interpretation of the system.

1

QUESTIONS OF INTERPRETATION OF THE CAPITALIST ECONOMY

M any of the concepts and arguments presented in the next chapters contrast with some past and present theories on economic growth and, in particular, on capitalist growth. The major schools of thought indirectly affected by my arguments will be the neoclassical school (Marshall, Walras, Wicksell) and its epigones, the neomarginalist school (Samuelson and Solow, to mention the best known). Many of my arguments against the neoclassical school are not original. They are necessary to provide the theoretical background of the reasoning and are useful also for a renewed attack on that school. In spite of the formidable criticisms to which it has been subject, many economists have continued to work on the marginalist model as if no such criticisms had taken place, raising that model to a degree of refinement which, high as it is, is most likely meaningless. On the other hand, since economics is a science in which little can be proved with numbers except in the very short run,[1] it is not absurd that contradictory theories should coexist. Indeed, this state of affairs may even be an advantage for the science, because it permits a continuous confrontation among different schools of thought.

I shall give a brief account of some of the discordant doctrines that have most to do with the subject of this book: a description of the long-term behavior of the capitalist system. This device may be useful not only to throw light on certain hypotheses on which many economic models have been built, but also to point out those elements which I think are most useful for the analysis of capitalist reality. The following brief description should not be taken as reflecting fully the thoughts of the authors quoted, nor as an attempt to reinterpret the history of economic thought.

THE CONTRADICTION OF MARGINALISTS
AND NEOMARGINALISTS

In the last forty years there has been more than one revolutionary in economics. The first was Sraffa,[2] who undermined the neo-

---

[1] The never solved index-number problem is a good example. See P. Samuelson, *Foundations of Economic Analysis* (Cambridge, Mass., 1953), pp. 146–63.

[2] P. Sraffa, "The Laws of Return under Competitive Conditions," *Economic Journal* (December, 1926).

classical edifice by proving that conditions of perfect competition cannot be reconciled with a meaningful interpretation of capitalism. The second was Keynes, who renovated the meaning and the language of economics, and whose ideas were subsequently used as a basis for general analyses of capitalism. A third revolution was initiated a few years ago by the "Cambridge school," which pointed out some logical faults imbedded in the marginalist constructions. The critique has not been fully digested by economic theorists. Perhaps one should even say that today's economics is twofaced: one face is made up of those authors who want to tackle the substance of the Cambridge criticism, either to accept or reject it; the other is made up of those who are wary of taking on this difficult problem, largely for fear of wasting time.

It is difficult to ascertain the paternity of the "Cambridge" revolution. One of the first references to the existence of a logical *non sequitur* in the marginalist scheme can be found in Mrs. Robinson's well-known essay, "The Production Function and the Theory of Capital."[3] Kaldor also tackled this question, saying that "the whole approach which regards the share of wages and of profits in output [in other words, the economy's production function] as being determined by the marginal rate of substitution between capital and labor . . . is hardly acceptable . . . as soon as it is realized that 'the marginal rate of substitution' . . . can only be determined once the rate of profits and the rate of wages are already known."[4] More recently, an Italian economist, P. Garegnani[5] has precisely identified the logical error. His analysis can be summarized as follows.

In the neoclassical model, "capital" is taken, *ex hypothesi*, as a *known* magnitude that specifies itself in *unknown* amounts of different capital goods; but capital is composed of physically different goods, and in order for it to be measured—and in order for the concept of marginal product to acquire meaning—it must be expressed in terms of *value*. For capital to be expressed in terms of

[3] J. Robinson, "The Production Function and the Theory of Capital," *Review of Economic Studies* (1953–54), especially pp. 81–85. Hints at a logical flaw in the marginalist scheme can also be found in Robinson, *An Essay on Marxian Economics* (London, 1947). The oral criticism of the marginal school, however, had been going on for some time in Cambridge.

[4] N. Kaldor, "Alternative Theories of Distribution," reprinted in his *Essays on Value and Distribution* (Glencoe, Ill., 1960).

[5] P. Garegnani, *Il capitale nelle teorie della distribuzione* (Milan, 1960).

value, however, the values of the individual capital goods composing the aggregate concept of capital must be known. Therefore,
the quantity of capital can be determined only when the values of
individual capital goods are known, and the values of individual
capital goods can be determined only when the quantity of capital
is known. Even if one starts from *given* quantities of individual
capital goods, the contradiction is not solved. In this case, the
quantity of capital is unknown, while the quantities of individual
capital goods are known. If the values of the individual capital
goods were also given, the value of capital (its quantity in an
homogeneous measure) would be known. However, if we consider
a situation in which the profit rates of capital goods are different—
not only a realistic possibility but also a necessary hypothesis
when dealing with *equilibrium* values, as the neoclassical theory
does—the law of uniformity of profit rates, brought about by competitive conditions in the market, dictates that equilibrium will be
reached through an increase in the services and quantities of those
capital goods with a higher profit rate, and a corresponding reduction of the services and quantities of capital goods on which the
profit rates are lower. But the quantities of capital goods were
given by definition: once it is admitted that they can change, they
are not known, and the notion of the quantity of capital disappears. Only if the quantity of capital goods were known—independent of the quantities of individual capital goods—would there
be no contradiction.[6] But this has been shown to be impossible.

This logical flaw affects all the marginalists' constructions. The
production function introduced by them[7] shows the relationship

---

[6] This summary follows the argument of C. Napoleoni, "Sulla teoria della
produzione come processo circolare," *Giornale degli economisti e annali di
economia* (January–February, 1961).

[7] A complete exposition of this analytical tool is given in the classical textbook of E. Schneider, *Pricing and Equilibrium, an Introduction to Static and
Dynamic Analysis* (London, 1952). Among the many descriptions, a simple and
straightforward one is that of J. M. Cassel, "On the Law of Variable Proportions," in W. Fellner and B. F. Haley (eds.), *Readings in the Theory of Income Distribution* (Philadelphia, 1957). A brief critical examination is contained in J. A. Schumpeter, *History of Economic Analysis* (Oxford, 1954),
P. IV, chap. vii, par. 8. The shape of the production function has been studied
extensively. For the purposes of the neoclassical equilibrium model, the function must be linear and homogeneous. The Cobb-Douglas function has these
properties; it is one of a general group of functions expressed as $x = Aa^\alpha b^\beta$,
in which $x =$ output, $a =$ labor, $b =$ capital, and α and β are the elasticities of
output to inputs of labor and capital. The function is homogeneous of $(\alpha + \beta)$

between product and the factors of production, labor and capital. The function orders alternative available techniques of production or combination of quantities of different inputs, but does not specify in which unit capital inputs should be measured. The neoclassical authors implicitly, and the neomarginalists explicitly,[8] believed that the production function represented not only a *technical* relationship between factors and product—expressed in physical terms—but also an *equilibrium* relationship, given factor prices, making it the relationship determining income distribution. They concluded that rather than being expressed at *given* factor prices and valid only *ex post facto*, the production function should be such that the marginal product of capital (and/or of labor) determines the rate of profits (and/or wages). Only in this way would the equilibrium system acquire also an *ex ante* validity. Having assumed this much, the problem of the neomarginalists was then only to identify the *form* of the function which would best represent equilibrium values.

All this is untenable because the factors' marginal product in terms of value can only be obtained at given prices and, therefore, at a given rate of profit. Moreover, it is impossible to establish what is the technical marginal product of the aggregate factor capital unless it is expressed in terms of value, or at given prices. Since the marginal product of capital in terms of value can only be calculated when the rate of profits is known, and since it should also determine the rate of profits, we face a contradiction which robs

---

degree: if $\alpha + \beta = 1$, the function is linear (constant returns to scale); if $\alpha + \beta < 1$ or $\alpha + \beta > 1$ there will be, respectively, increasing or decreasing returns to scale. The marginal rate of substitution is expressed by $\alpha b / \beta a$. Cf. C. W. Cobb and P. H. Douglas, "A Theory of Production," *American Economic Review* (March, 1928), and Douglas, "Are There Laws of Production?," *ibid* (March, 1948). Aside from the Cobb-Douglas function, other functions have been studied and applied to data referring to individual enterprises or to the economy as a whole. However, the statistical applications undertaken to test one or another shape of the production function face considerable difficulties. Research based on time series must compare values through time by the (inevitable) use of index numbers. Research based on cross-sectional data cannot provide explanations of the dynamic aspects of the production function: it can only describe what happens in a given moment, without identifying causes or consequences. Lacking interpretative ability, these studies have often had to rely on a neoclassical free competition model. See A. A. Walters, "Production and Cost Functions: An Econometric Survey," in *Econometrica* (January–April, 1963).

[8] In particular the "American school"; see below, p. 8, n. 11.

the production function and the general equilibrium theory of their persuasiveness.

These considerations eliminate the possibility of using the production function as an instrument to reveal the mode of income distribution at the level of the economy as a whole. The mutual links between income distribution and economic growth, a central relationship,[9] are seriously undermined.

One could object that, if all this critique does is to prove the impossibility of measuring capital, no important principle in the marginalist argument would have to be sacrificed. Even if the quantity of capital cannot be measured at the level of the economy, each entrepreneur finds it possible, at a given moment of time, to picture the production function facing his enterprise; otherwise, he would not be able to make any decision. A plausible extension of this principle would be to make it valid for the economy as a whole. In this way, the rules which, according to the marginalists, determine profit and wage rates acquire validity as extensions of the rules which can be applied successfully at the level of each individual enterprise, even though it is impossible to establish them directly for the economy as a whole.

Unfortunately, this extension is not admissible. The neoclassical argument gave rise to an equilibrium theory—a "natural equilibrium" deriving from the internal features of the model. As was indicated above, the circular reasoning underlying the idea of the measurability of capital destroys the interpretative capabilities of that theory. This means that it is impossible to reconstruct a "natural" scale of values originating from within that model. When one considers the economy as a whole, one cannot deny the existence of some relationship between factors of production on one side and output on the other. But a number of questions cannot be answered within the marginalist model: what the form of this relationship is, in what way changes in profits and salaries influence it, and how it is affected by technical progress. Moreover, even at

[9] Ricardo wrote: "Political Economy . . . should be . . . an enquiry into the laws which determine the division of the produce of industry amongst the classes who concur in its formation. No law can be laid down respecting quantity but a tolerably correct one can be laid down respecting proportions . . . the latter [is] the true object of the science . . ." (letter to Malthus of October 9, 1820, in *Works and Correspondence of David Ricardo*, ed. P. Sraffa [10 vols.; Cambridge, 1951], Vol. VIII).

the level of the individual business the production function ceases to have much meaning.[10] What conclusion could be derived from studying one such enterprise when nothing is known of the whole of which it is a part?

In spite of all this, many economists, particularly the "American school," have continued to present problems and build models based on the production function.[11] Even in applied economics, the critique mentioned above has not had much effect. A great number of analyses concerning longer periods and aggregate quantities and based on the marginalists' concepts continue to be made by governments, research institutes, and financial entities. These studies and models argue *as if* there exists a way of measuring capital. However, it is not permissible to postulate any measure whatever, since the validity of the analysis depends to a large extent on the validity of the measure. In economics, where the interdependence of phenomena plays such an overwhelming role, to assume any measure constitutes an incomplete analysis of the factual evidence. Unless the contrary can be proved, there will always be doubt as to whether the measure chosen would really remain fixed if *all* other economic patterns should change.

This is not the only weakness of the marginalist theories. Since their framework of analysis is still the static general equilibrium scheme, they possess many of the limitations of that scheme. One important limitation is the assumption, rarely made explicit, of a

[10] Without taking account of the great discussion on market forms, which in the last quarter of a century has revolutionized enterprise economics.

[11] The literature is vast, and only a few important titles will be mentioned: N. Georgescu-Roegen, "The Aggregate Production Function and Its Application to the Von Neumann Economic Model," chap. IV of T. C. Koopmans (ed.), *Activity Analysis of Production and Allocation* (New York, 1951); R. M. Solow, "The Production Function and the Theory of Capital," *Review of Economic Studies* (1955–56); Samuelson and Solow, "A Complete Capital Model Involving Heterogeneous Capital Goods," *Quarterly Journal of Economics* (November, 1956); Solow, "Technical Change and the Aggregate Production Function," *Review of Economics and Statistics* (August, 1957); Solow, "Investment and Technical Progress," in K. J. Arrow *et al.* (eds.), *Mathematical Methods in the Social Sciences, 1959 Proceedings* (Stanford Symposium on Mathematical Methods in the Social Sciences; Stanford, Calif., 1959); Arrow, H. B. Chenery, B. S. Minhas, and Solow, "Capital Labor Substitution and Economic Efficiency," *Review of Economics and Statistics* (August, 1961); see also R. Dorfman, Samuelson, and Solow, *Linear Programming and Economic Analysis* (New York, 1958), pp. 204–346, for an exposition in a dynamic setting. Samuelson seems (implicitly) to have had some doubts about the neoclassical model; see "Parable and Realism in Capital Theory: The Surrogate Production Function," *Review of Economic Studies* (June, 1962).

constant pattern of consumption. When the general equilibrium model was put in dynamic terms,[12] it became necessary to assume equiproportionate sectoral growth, the peculiarity of which assumption is that the initial and final composition of output are equal. As a result, the marginalist is prevented from studying the links between the growth of output, the change in the composition of consumption, and the change in the composition of output. Since these are central questions of economic dynamics, marginalist theories do not provide an adequate theoretical structure—even apart from the flaw in their logic regarding the measurement of capital.

It is now clear why it is necessary to re-examine critically the main features of the capitalist system in order to see what really determines its structure and the direction of its development. It will not seem strange, therefore, that the starting point in this search is another look at the classics, in particular Ricardo and Marx.

THE PROBLEM OF VALUE ACCORDING TO RICARDO AND MARX

Classical economists regarded the measurement problem of fundamental importance for the understanding of economic phenomena and for the interpretation of the economic system. For them, the problem was essentially that of finding a fixed measure of value, rather than of capital.[13] When they limit themselves to the study of a "natural" economy, or a system in which there exists only one productive sector which employs as capital its only product (for example, agriculture and wheat) and in which wages and salaries, expressed in terms of that product, are fixed at the level of physiological subsistence, it is easy to measure the total output of the economy and its distribution, since quantity and value measures are identical. In this system profits are taken as a surplus. But when this simplified scheme is abandoned and different types of capital goods are introduced, classical economists had to have recourse to a measure of value which specified both total output and its composition.

In equilibrium, for each commodity this measure of value must equal its price. For Ricardo, the equilibrium price of a commodity

---

[12] J. Von Neumann, "A Model of General Economic Equilibrium," *Review of Economic Studies* (1945–46).

[13] For a clear over-all picture, see Mrs. Robinson's "Marx, Marshall and Keynes," in her *Collected Economic Papers* (Oxford, 1960), Vol. II.

is composed of the sum of wages and profits paid in the production of a commodity, both calculated at their equilibrium rates. Wage rates tend toward uniformity in the production of different commodities as a result of competitive forces on the labor market. If the percentage of the price represented by wages and profits were the same for all commodities, the equilibrium exchange rate between two commodities would equal the ratio between their production costs as well as the ratio between the man-hours expended in the production of each commodity, since wages are uniform. For Ricardo, the quantity of embodied labor is the true measure of value. However, if the share of wages and profits in the price of different commodities is not the same everywhere, commodities do not tend to exchange each other on the basis of the quantity of labor embodied in each of them. This difficulty can be observed from a different viewpoint. Since the labor-output ratio is different in each industry, the prices of commodities produced by different industries will be different; and since profit rates, like wage rates, tend toward uniformity as a result of competition, where the ratio is higher prices will be higher. Within Ricardo's framework, let us assume that the wage rate has declined over the whole economy. Entrepreneurs will then save more in industries where the labor-output ratio is high than in industries where that ratio is low. Since profit rates are uniform, commodity prices will have to change in inverse proportion to the amount of labor required for each commodity, but the quantity of labor has not changed, and prices will no longer reflect the quantity of labor. Of course, a decline in wages will affect the ratio of labor to capital employed in the production of each commodity, and a new equilibrium will of necessity show differences in the amount of labor. Whether the prices and the quantities of labor found in this new equilibrium will again "correspond," as they did in the previous equilibrium, can only be ascertained if either the wage rate or the profit rate is specified. There is no assurance that the value relationship of the old equilibrium will obtain in the new equilibrium. Continuity is lacking, and the system of values may well change in time.

The same difficulty is found in Marx,[14] even though his model improves many of Ricardo's concepts and enlarges its vision. From

[14] A now classical exposition of the Marxian system and of its problems is that of P. M. Sweezy, *The Theory of Capitalist Development* (New York, 1942).

his formula of total output, composed of the values of constant capital, variable capital, and the surplus, Marx obtains the three fundamental ratios of the capitalist system: the rate of surplus value, which is the ratio of surplus value to variable capital; the organic composition of capital, which is the ratio of constant to total capital (the sum of constant and variable capital); and the rate of profits, which is the ratio of surplus value to total capital.[15] Marx believed, as did all classical and neoclassical economists, that the forces of competition on the market make the rates of profits and of surplus value tend toward uniformity among the different branches of production. Thus, if these rates are equal in all sectors of production, the organic composition of capital must also be equal everywhere, since value is completely used up among these three elements and since any one of these ratios can be obtained when the other two are known. However, while the forces of competition determine the uniformity of the rate of profits and of surplus value in Marx's framework, they cannot also influence the organic composition of capital. This cannot be determined at will by entrepreneurs but derives merely from the physical, chemical, or mechanical properties of the production technique in use at each moment of time, which are non-economic data.[16] Not even the Marxian law of value, therefore, gives the invariable measure of value. Marx himself was aware of this difficulty, which he called the problem of the correspondence of values to prices.[17]

[15] These ratios have been translated into modern economic language by Mrs. Robinson in *Marxian Economics*, pp. 6–9.

[16] Below it will be shown why entrepreneurs cannot determine the character of the technology for the economy as a whole (see p. 84).

[17] Sweezy's defense of the Marxian definition of value seems weak. He argues that "it is perfectly legitimate to postulate a capitalist system in which organic compositions of capital are everywhere equal and hence the law of value does hold, and to examine the functioning of such a system" (*Capitalist Development*, p. 70). However, in the Marxian model the organic composition of capital must be uniform, otherwise the law of value fails, and a law of value only 99 per cent valid is not admissible. In other words, if the organic compositions of capital in reality are differentiated, one would use the wrong measure—and would therefore make the wrong interpretations—if the measure had been built on the basis of uniform organic compositions. A similar argument has been used by M. H. Dobb, *On Economic Theory and Socialism* (London, 1955), pp. 194–95. It is interesting to note that the defense of the neoclassical model is conducted along similar lines: measuring capital is impossible, but it is possible to elaborate statistical tools which can approximate it; see J. R. Hicks, "The Measurement of Capital in Relation to the Measurement of Other Economic Aggregates," in F. A. Lutz and D. C. Hague (eds.), *The Theory of Capital* (New York, 1961). Sraffa, in discussing

These are not the only contradictions present in the theories of the classical economists. There is also considerable difficulty, particularly in the Marxian scheme, in reconciling the notion of a competitive market as a meeting place of independent economic operators, in which there is a uniform profit rate, with the notion of the dependence of consumption on production, an aspect of the capitalist system that was necessary in Marx's thought to provide a goal for the process of formation of surplus value (and which was also present in other classical doctrines). It is well known that if production determines consumption, in the sense that consumer tastes as expressed are determined by production choices made by entrepreneurs, demand will not be independent from supply. Thus, the price of a commodity will not be the price resulting from a competitive market, in which independent schedules of demand and supply prices meet.

Concluding these remarks, I would like to suggest that both the classical and the marginal schools become contradictory when they introduce *a uniform profit rate throughout the economy*. This hypothesis is accompanied, in the classical model, by the breaking down of the correspondence between prices and values, and in the neoclassical model by the impossibility of measuring the value of capital and also, in this case, by the breaking down of the price-value correspondence. In fact, the criticism of the neoclassical doctrine referred to above, which is based on the impossibility of measuring the value of capital satisfactorily, is similar to the general problem of an unchanging measure of value as raised by Ricardo. What a labor-value measure was for the classical economists, a determinate price system is for the neoclassical economists. But the impossibility of measuring capital in terms of value implies the absence of a value measure not only for capital, but for all economic factors and outputs, since capital is used in the production of them all.

RECENT ATTEMPTS TO RECONSTRUCT A DETERMINATE MODEL

The classical model, although just as greatly affected by a logical flaw as is the neoclassical model, perhaps offers a more solid

---

Hicks's paper (p. 305 of the same volume), points out that the measures used by statisticians are necessarily approximate and provide an area where the index-number problem can be tackled; theoretical measures, however, require absolute precision: any imperfection not only disturbs but destroys the theoretical basis of a model.

foundation upon which to construct a valid interpretation of the workings of the capitalist system. The classicists were generally the more interested in long-term economic analysis, and their picture of the dynamic aspects of reality is far better than is the mythical equilibrium of the marginalists. In fact, some of the recent attempts to offer an alternative interpretation of the process of capitalist development are based on the classical model. Among these, the most important and worthy of attention are, in my opinion, the attempts of Mrs. Robinson, Kaldor, and Sraffa.

Mrs. Robinson's model[18] is by now well known, and I shall not summarize it. In my view, the model produces many original concepts and results but suffers from some of the defects already present in the neoclassical analysis. Mrs. Robinson considers the problem of a true measure of value impossible to solve. But on the basis of a number of simplifying assumptions which permit the construction of a system in dynamic equilibrium (what she calls the "golden age"), she finds it possible to compare different economies at any given time and the same economy at different moments of time. The model's equilibrium, however, depends exclusively on the restrictive assumptions used in its definition and does not appear to be able to maintain itself if the assumptions are changed. In fact, Mrs. Robinson takes great care to point out that the system is unstable and that its growth is not warranted by the laws that underlie its structure. One has the impression, in following the working of the model, that the existence and the continuity of capitalism happen almost in spite of the will and the nature of men.

Let us briefly consider a few of the principal assumptions of Mrs. Robinson's model. First, the assumption of uniformity of rates of profit in the different sectors of production: even though she sees a progressive increase of industrial concentration in the long run, the assumption of the uniformity of profit rates is not changed, which is contradictory because the existence of monopolistic structures cannot be justified unless varying rates of profit exist on the market. A second assumption of the model is the existence of a mechanism by which relative changes in the rates of profits and in wage rates determine, in the long run, changes in production techniques. As a consequence, techniques will be more

[18] Robinson, "Production Function," and *The Accumulation of Capital* (London, 1956). Mrs. Robinson has developed her model in many other publications; the most important are included in *Collected Economic Papers*.

or less "mechanized," or use a higher or lower proportion of capital. According to Mrs. Robinson, there exists at each moment of time an entire "spectrum" of alternative techniques. A third assumption is of technical progress, which changes the spectrum of techniques independent of any variation in the rate of profits and of wages. Each time technical progress occurs, it creates a new spectrum of alternative techniques, among which entrepreneurs will again make a choice, depending on the relative changes in rates and profits and wages. The last two elements seem to be a reformulation of the neoclassical production function, at least in its technological aspect.

In passing, it may be worth while to note that historians of economic thought have not attempted to discover why the concept of alternative production techniques—an undemonstrated assumption, as we shall see—has arisen in economics. In the work of the classical economists, the place occupied by this postulate has been either relatively small or non-existent. In the constructions of neoclassical and contemporary economists it constitutes the basic infrastructure of economic thought.

Finally, Mrs. Robinson introduces the idea of technical progress with different degrees of capital intensity, but does not try to explain the reasons or the laws that determine the occurrence of this or that degree of capital intensity.

The model also assumes the constant composition of consumption in time and with a rise in income. This assumption is necessary in order to give a comparable evaluation of output through time, which, in turn, is required in order to measure both alternative techniques of production and the effects of technical progress. The assumption is present in all recent growth models, where it is treated as a convenient way of simplifying what are considered to be minor complications, which can later be reintroduced in the model to make it more realistic. Unfortunately, those complications are far from being of minor importance, a point which will be developed below. At this stage it is sufficient to recall that, if economic growth is defined as the increase in per capita income, and therefore in per capita consumption, such an increase must occur (1) as an increase in the consumption of existing commodities; (2) as an increase in the consumption of some commodities at a faster or slower rate than the increase in the consumption of other commodities; and (3) as a consumption of new commodities. If the definition of economic growth did not include all these cases, it would contradict a fundamental postulate of economics, according to which consumers do not derive the same "satisfaction" ("utility," pleasure) from consuming each successive "unit" of a commodity.

In contrast with the method followed by Mrs. Robinson, Kaldor[19] abandons completely the mechanism of the production function. According to him, "technical progress and capital accumulation proceed together and it is not possible to distinguish the effects of the latter from the effects of the former." In fact, "the use of more capital per worker inevitably entails the introduction of superior techniques. . . ."[20] Although well aware of the problem of measuring capital, Kaldor does not attempt to solve it and adopts in his model "any physical measure"—weight of steel per man, for example, which is clearly not an unchanging measure and therefore is open to the same criticism to which he subjects the neomarginalist theories.[21] Kaldor also maintains the hypotheses of the constant composition of consumption and of the uniformity of rates of profit.

Sraffa's recent contribution, more than any other, approaches a solution of the problem of an unchanging measure.[22] Sraffa's treatment is essentially classical in method and outlook. He considers an economic system in a state of "reproduction," that is, a perfectly circular system in which the same commodities appear as both outputs and inputs. The system produces a surplus of outputs over inputs. The profit rate is uniform in all sectors of production. Wages—also uniform throughout the economy—are composed in part of subsistence commodities, thus becoming a purely technical input of the production process, and in part of the commodities

[19] In a number of papers; see "A Model of Economic Growth," *Economic Journal* (December, 1957), reprinted in *Essays in Economic Stability and Growth* (Glencoe, Ill., 1960); "Economic Growth and the Problem of Inflation," *Economica* (August, 1959); "Capital Accumulation and Economic Growth," in Lutz and Hague (eds.), *The Theory of Capital*; "A New Model of Economic Growth," *Review of Economic Studies* (June, 1962) (with J. A. Mirrlees).

[20] Kaldor, "A Model," p. 264 of the reprint.

[21] In his most recent model ("A New Model," p. 174), Kaldor tries to avoid the problem of measuring capital by using the value of current investment, but the use of this concept seems awkward when describing long-run phenomena and, in particular, when talking of entrepreneurial expectations.

[22] Sraffa, *Production of Commodities by Means of Commodities: Prelude to a Critique of Economic Theory* (Cambridge, 1960). Sraffa's interest in these problems was already evident in his Introduction to *Works and Correspondence of David Ricardo*.

included in the surplus, thus becoming also a part of the net product of the system. On the basis of this model, Sraffa arrives, in an original way, at a measure of value. The measure is constructed as a composite commodity—the standard commodity—produced by a standard system, in which the commodity composition is the same for both output and inputs. The standard system can always be obtained from an actual system by divesting the latter of its "excess" in relation to the former. In the actual economic system, the rates of profit expressed in terms of *quantity* (either of commodities or of the labor embodied in them) are not necessarily uniform because the different commodities, in terms of quantities, do not appear in the sum of inputs in the same proportion as they appear in the sum of outputs. Prices of commodities must thus be such as to make profit rates uniform *in terms of value*. On the other hand, the rate of profits in the standard economic system is uniform in terms of quantity (because of its peculiar proportions), without recourse to prices. As Sraffa puts it, "The same rate of profits, which in the standard system is obtained as a ratio between *quantities* of commodities, will in the actual system result from the ratio of aggregate *values*."[23] Because of the ever-present possibility of reducing the actual system to the standard system, the standard commodity—which derives from the standard system—also represents the unchanging measure for the actual system.[24]

To obtain these results Sraffa has had to sacrifice a great deal. It has already been pointed out[25] that he does not allow demand to play any role in his model. Demand is not absent from the system; it is taken as *given* or, rather, the model is abstracted from demand functions. Insofar as wages are part of the means of production, they are only subsistence wages and a technical input of production, and the demand which they give rise to can correctly be taken as given without stretching reality. But insofar as wages are part of the social surplus (of the net product), they can no longer be considered a technical element in production. The composition of de-

[23] Sraffa, *Production of Commodities*, p. 23.

[24] A similar procedure could perhaps be applied to the Marxian system; the standard system does not seem very dissimilar from a model in which the organic compositions of capital are uniform.

[25] Along with Napoleoni ("Sulla teoria della produzione"), R. F. Harrod, in "Production of Commodities by Means of Commodities, a Review Article" (*Economic Journal* [December, 1961]), makes this observation. See also V. Dominedò, "Una teoria economica ricardiana," *Giornale degli economisti e annali di economia* (November–December, 1962).

mand should, as a result, cease to be fixed, unless an assumption of constant composition of net product is introduced. In fact, this assumption has been explicitly made by Sraffa.

These restrictions on the model[26] prevent its utilization for interpretative purposes, even though all the neoclassical bottlenecks have been unstopped. First, to take demand as given means that production dominates the economic process, but this corollary (of a hypothesis, not of a theorem) is not discussed by Sraffa. Second, his unchanging measure is applied to an economy with a uniform rate of profit, a characteristic which limits the system to a static point of view, as we shall see below. Third, the model assumes competitive conditions, and this assumption may contradict the recognition, implicit in every objective analysis such as Sraffa's, that supply determines demand.

If the attempt to construct a fixed measure of value is not an unqualified success, the major merit of Sraffa's research, in my opinion, is his demonstration that variations in relative prices, observable when the means of production are expressed in terms of the quantity of labor they represent at different moments of time and with production techniques held constant, "cannot be reconciled with *any* notion of capital as a measurable quantity independently of distribution and prices."[27] This result is relevant for the following analysis, wherein the problem of measuring capital will not be considered as separate from the general problem of measuring value.

CONCLUSION

In this chapter I have tried to single out certain points that are relevant for an interpretation of the capitalist system. In summary, they are (1) the difficulty of measuring value through time; (2) the hypothesis of a uniform profit rate prevailing throughout the economy; (3) the hypothesis of a constant composition of consumption,

[26] In Sraffa's theoretical framework, directed toward the analysis of purely objective relationships of a productive system seen *in vacuo* in order to determine the relationships between income distribution, prices, and value, those restrictions are perfectly legitimate. However, for the interpretation of economic growth, Sraffa's model does not seem particularly fruitful, unless the model's relationships are utilized in a dynamic context, and I cannot undertake such a task here. However, it will be shown below that the problem of measuring values, in a dynamic setting and in heuristic exercises, is not solvable by means of objective procedures.

[27] Sraffa, *Production of Commodities*, p. 38.

found in both old and new interpretations of the economic system; (4) the hypothesis of competitive conditions as an expositional device in model-building; and (5) the hypothesis of alternative techniques from which to choose, according to the rates of profits and of wages prevailing at each moment of time.

2

A SIMPLIFIED MODEL: DEFINITIONS AND RESTRICTIVE ASSUMPTIONS

I am unable to construct a model that is both complete and wholly consistent. In the following chapters, therefore, the reader will have to bear with the difficulty of facing a model that does not illustrate all the aspects of the capitalist economic system, although it aims at a general interpretation. This is in part inevitable with a model, irrespective of the magnitude of the task to be undertaken. Without certain restrictive assumptions, the subject matter becomes a confused reproduction of reality, too complex to be analyzed. In any case, the present effort is an exercise in interpretation, rather than in forecasting. The distinction is worth making, and our simplified model should be judged in terms of the first rather than the second objective. This is also the reason why the reader is invited to consider with patience the rather primitive treatment to which some of the variables in the model will be subjected (e.g., the propensity to save, the life span of machinery, the character of technical progress).

Some of the assumptions are in these pages introduced only to facilitate the writer's task; others should be more appropriately considered as postulates; still others are temporary assumptions, to be abandoned later in the analysis. On the other hand, not all the assumptions underlying the model will be identified. It is necessary to leave this task to the reader and let him determine which assumptions have not been made explicit in the course of the argument. This peculiar behavior is frequent in economics. A more complete formal description of the assumptions would not leave any space for the substantive part of the argument. Many of the hypotheses introduced cannot be considered completely neutral, in the sense that their presence or absence has no significant influence on the characteristics of the capitalist system. I am well aware that I may have made mistakes in the choice of assumptions and simplified too much or inappropriately.

THE TIME HORIZON

In examining the conditions of the growth process, economists have never changed their time horizon. The distinction between short and long periods has not been challenged since it was introduced by Marshall. The short period can be defined, very simply, as that time span during which the productive capacity of the enterprise or of the economy, according to the point of view being taken, does not change.[1] The long period can be defined as that time span in which productive capacity does change.

This distinction did not exist in the models of classical authors, for whom the short period—in its Marshallian meaning—had relatively little importance. They did not usually analyze changes in composition of the factors of production at each moment of time, but rather studied problems of general equilibrium in the long-period frame of reference. For example, Marx worked on the assumption of only one possible combination of capital and labor. Ricardo considered changes in population growth—a long-term phenomenon, as a re-equilibrating factor.

The Marshallian distinction appears inadequate when we are dealing with economic growth and capitalist structure. The short period, in which productive capacity does not change, cannot be utilized in the analysis of development, where by definition only the variations in productive capacity and in conditions of production are relevant. Since the short period cannot be utilized, development economics loses its time dimension, and the treatment of the pace of development becomes confusing. Excluded from the short period, the development process can only be seen within the indefinite time horizon of the Marshallian long period, which has no relation to the nature of dynamic phenomena and, therefore, is of little help in interpreting an evolving economy. Yet the periods of development must somehow be distinguished if we wish to identify their fundamental characteristics. Without a definite time frame, there is a risk of confusing permanent with temporary phenomena, of blurring the distinction between fundamental and random changes, and of disregarding the historical limitations of the system under study.

The Marshallian distinction between short and long periods is

---

[1] For the current definition of short period, see A. W. Stonier and D. C. Hague, *A Textbook of Economic Theory* (London, 1953), pp. 108, 153. For them the short period is "a period of time within which the firm can only increase output by hiring more labor and buying more raw materials [while] the capital equipment of the firm cannot be altered," or "a period which [is] long enough for supplies of a commodity to be altered by increases or decreases in current output, but not long enough for the fixed equipment producing this output to be adapted to produce larger or smaller outputs."

therefore not used in these pages. The long period is defined here as that time span in which the quantity and the nature of the commodities which constitute the subsistence level of consumption can change. The short period is that time span in which the quantity and the nature of the commodities which constitute the subsistence level of consumption do not change. This short period is thus longer than the Marshallian short term, and changes in the productive capacity of the enterprise, as well as of the economy, will normally occur within it.

The key to my definition is the level of subsistence. This can be simply defined as that level of income which is just high enough to allow the labor force to maintain and reproduce itself.[2] With the rise in income and a sufficiently long period of time, social and psychological conditions change to such an extent that the level of consumption becomes irreversible, even though it may be well above the necessary physiological minimum. I therefore postulate the existence, at each moment of time, of a consumption level higher than the biological minimum, which is the minimum in a psychological sense.[3]

In practice, the psychological minimum is easily identifiable when one compares advanced systems, such as that of the United States, with backward economies. This is also confirmed by the fact that a deep change in economic and social structures accompanies the increase in the psychological minimum. As an example, it would not be possible to take away cars from American workers today without causing a crisis in the system, even though the car is far from being a necessary physiological item in consumer budgets. This is so not only because the car is now a part of the psychological minimum consumption of individuals, but also because the car has become, for many people, the only available means of

[2] The subsistence level can be referred to consumption as well as to income, since at that level savings can be disregarded. The subsistence level includes also the consumption (income) necessary to increase the labor force.

[3] One could, for the sake of realism, suggest that even though the subsistence level of consumption does change as time and income progress, any reduction in it should create less of a crisis when the economy has attained the level of psychological subsistence than when it is at the level of biological subsistence. As a result, the capitalist system would gain in flexibility. However, no such conclusion can in fact be drawn: political scientists have made a number of observations showing that crises (such as revolutions) are more likely to occur after the biological subsistence level is exceeded. Political awareness is very near zero when people live at starvation or near-starvation levels.

transportation. This in turn has radically changed the pattern of other consumption (its effect can be seen, for example, in suburbia).[4]

In the following pages, a change in the subsistence level of consumption will be related not to the average consumption of the community but to the consumption of the lower income class of the community. In this way, one avoids confusion between the biological and psychological levels of subsistence.[5] Since the play of economic factors is significantly different at and beyond the biological level of subsistence, this definition avoids situations in which some classes of consumers have passed the biological level of subsistence while others are still at it.[6]

The observation that the level of subsistence is variable is not new in the economic literature. Mrs. Robinson has utilized a similar concept, which she calls the "inflation barrier."[7] What goes under the name of "ratchet effect" in the theory of business cycles[8] is another way of expressing the same hypothesis. The ratchet effect is the phenomenon by which the proportion consumed out of income is a function of the ratio between current income and the highest income received in the past. In other words, the cyclical behavior of the economy transforms the habits of individual consumers, after they have experienced a high level of income, in such a way that in the future they tend to consume more or to reduce their consumption less drastically.

This essay primarily studies the long period, as defined above. The short period will be dealt with when the development of production is described, mainly to show how the elements that are introduced in the model behave in the time horizon chosen by

---

[4] J. Robinson, in "Marxism, Religion and Science" (*Monthly Review* [December, 1962], p. 430), discards this possibility without discussing it (on the other hand, cf. n. 7 below).

[5] This assumption is, of course, unrealistic: even in advanced economies there are today classes which have not yet exceeded the biological subsistence level, while others have been above it for a long time.

[6] If our model were not divided into classes (see p. 25), and if we were to examine in isolation the phenomena of consumption and of savings, the concept of variable subsistence should also be reformulated.

[7] *Accumulation of Capital*, pp. 48–50.

[8] This idea must be attributed to both J. S. Duesenberry (*Income, Saving and the Theory of Consumer Behavior* [Cambridge, Mass., 1949], pp. 69–92, 114–16) and to F. Modigliani ("Fluctuations in the Saving-Income Ratio: A Problem in Economic Forecasting," in *Studies in Income and Wealth* [New York, 1949], Vol. XI, pp. 371–443).

modern economics. The development of capitalist production does, of course, have relevance in the long period, since the determination of equilibrium in one time horizon influences the determination of equilibrium in the other time horizon.

SOCIETY AND CLASSES

In order to reduce the capitalist system to its essential characteristics, society is arbitrarily divided into two classes: entrepreneur-capitalists, who save and invest all their income,[9] which is totally derived from profits; and workers, who consume all their income, which is totally derived from wages. Profits, savings, and investment thus become identical quantities.[10] This assumption, certainly unrealistic in a world composed of a great variety of classes and social groupings, is commonly adopted in the economic literature. It can be easily discarded in favor of a more complex structure, but the model would become too complicated for our purpose. Moreover, any greater refinement of what I believe to be the essential simplicity of class relationships in capitalism can seriously confuse an interpretative effort.

The last statement may need clarification. The choice made here is not ideological. Rather, it flows from the evidence presented by much economic analysis, acording to which economic phenomena of only minor relevance arise from including a greater number of social groups in the analysis. In addition, there is a logical necessity in our choice. Either one keeps the number of classes to a minimum, studies their significance, and tries to interpret their interplay, or one is forced to construct an n-class model, in which any law concerning the relationships between classes is bound to be submerged by the number of cases. A few studies have shown that when an n-class model is chosen, the analysis tends to become typological rather than interpretative.[11]

The distinction between capitalists (*rentiers*) on one side and

---

[9] For our purposes, it would be sufficient to assume as constant the propensity of entrepreneurs to consume.

[10] This is not an uncommon assumption. A. K. Sen ("Neo-Classical and Neo-Keynesian Theories of Distribution," *Economic Record* [March, 1963]) has shown that the neomarginalist model assumes perfect foresight of entrepreneurs and eliminates an independent investment function.

[11] See, for example, J. Marchal and J. Lecaillon, *La repartition du revenu national* (Paris, 1958).

entrepreneurs (managers) on the other will be avoided. Also, the fact that incomes of workers are a mixture of profits and wages, because of the choice open to them of either consuming or investing their income, will be disregarded. The labor force will be considered to be homogeneous, so that the wage rate can be taken as uniform in all branches of production. Alternatively, one could assume that wage rates are differentiated and that they depend upon the degree of specialization of the worker or on the amount spent for his training. This assumption, common to almost all economic literature, is unrealistic because a greater degree of specialization is often associated with a greater bargaining power and, consequently, with monopolistic elements in the labor market. However, it will be shown that the introduction into the model of differentiated wage rates does not have an important effect.

It will be assumed here that the wage rate equals the subsistence level of income (psychological subsistence level); this assumption will no longer hold in Chapter 5, when the working of the capitalist system at the level of an aggregative model is examined. Wages, thus, are not part of the economy's net income but are considered a purely technical input of production. In this way, profits become a simple residue and equal the economy's net income. However, since the subsistence wage changes in the long run, the present treatment will not be essentially different from that followed by the large majority of economists who include a part of the wage bill in net output.

SECTORS OF PRODUCTION

This analysis is developed on different levels of simplification. On the one hand, in examining the structure of profit rates, disaggregated and simplified situations are set up; on the other hand, in examining the deployment of capitalist production, an aggregative model is used. In order to investigate certain relationships pertaining to the latter, the economy has been arbitrarily divided into two sectors: the sector producing investment goods (sector K), and the sector producing consumer goods (sector C). Since workers do not save and entrepreneurs do not consume, the total wage bill paid in both sectors equals the output of sector C. The surplus accruing to sector C, after the sector's own wage bill is paid, equals the wage bill in sector K. The importance of the distinction between sectors K and C, for the purpose of this analysis, diminishes as soon as the neutral character of technical progress is established.

The study of the structure of profit rates, which has an important role in the determination of values and of the price system, must be conducted at a level of simplification different from that used in the study of the capitalistic process of production. This distinction does not affect the working of the model because the "average" rate of profits is not influenced in any particular way (see below, Chapter 3).

NATURAL RESOURCES AND POPULATION

The study of the model is limited to its behavior in a "closed" system, that of a perfectly self-sufficient economy, without any relationship to other economies. It is therefore necessary to assume that natural resources (mineral, physical, and so on) are uniformly distributed over the territory of the economy under consideration, and that they do not give a particular bias to the growth process. In any case, when examining development of a closed economy through time, the amount of natural resources will be considered as given. Economic phenomena deriving from special configurations of the space in which a system happens to be located will not be discussed. They are important but do not influence the interpretation of capitalism presented here. The reader is therefore asked to picture for himself an economic world without space. In dealing with certain aspects of an open economy (see Appendix A), these assumptions will be reconsidered.

Population is taken as an exogenous factor. I do not consider the way in which the rate of change in population is influenced by other economic factors.[12] In the course of the analysis, it is assumed that population remains unchanged in order to simplify the exposition.

TECHNICAL CONDITIONS OF PRODUCTION

There will be many references in these pages to a technique of production being used by the economy as a whole. This expression stands for the complex of productive processes that characterize an economy at each moment of time. The technique, or complex of techniques, being used at each moment to produce a given output

---

[12] D. C. Paige ("Economic Growth: The Last Hundred Years," *National Institute Economic Review* [July, 1961]) concludes a statistical inquiry by stating that there is no clear relationship between the increase in population and the growth of the economy.

must be such as to furnish a surplus of commodities over and above the quantities absorbed by the means of production, including the (physiological and psychological) subsistence level of wages. It is assumed that the subsistence level of wages is never so high as to reduce to zero the surplus obtainable with a given technique.

A tentative proof that there exists only one possible production technique in each branch of production at each moment of time will be offered. The case in which there are many alternative techniques from which entrepreneurs can choose according to the relative changes in the rates of profits and of wages will be disregarded. Therefore, the model does not admit a production function. If there exists only one rigid combination of factors of production in each sector of production, the concepts of the marginal product of capital and of labor—even if the problem of their measurement could be solved—lose their meaning. It will be assumed that each technique produces only one commodity, and that each commodity is produced by only one technique. Joint products and joint production processes will not be analyzed.

As time goes on, techniques of production change by virtue of technical progress. This phenomenon will be analyzed below; at this point, it will be sufficient to point out that technical progress consists of the introduction of new techniques (innovations and improvements of a technical, scientific, and organizational character) that are preferred, in all circumstances, to techniques previously adopted. For the moment, it is assumed that technical progress spreads evenly over the different sectors of production, so as to leave their mutual relationships unchanged.

In discussing technical progress, I will limit its impact to productive processes. The questions arising from the inclusion, under the phenomenon of technical progress, of improvements in consumer goods will not be tackled. On the other hand, the present study cannot abstain from introducing "new" products into the analysis. These are regarded, therefore, as new but not better products—an extremely awkward assumption. The notion of new products also encompasses any change in the nature, form, and quality of existing commodities.

Land is not included among the factors of production. It is considered as a free commodity, not subject to pricing.

The period of production, or the time elapsed between the be-

ginning and the completion of the production process of a commodity, is considered as constant or as changing proportionately in
all branches of production as time goes on and as techniques
change. The same assumption is made for the "gestation" period
of investment.

In working with a dynamic model, the necessary depreciation of
means of production poses considerable difficulties, particularly
when the introduction of new techniques has the effect of changing
the economic life span of existing plants. In order to simplify the
model, it will be assumed that the rate at which the different means
of production depreciate—in the long run and in the presence of
a great number of innovations—remains constant. Alternatively,
it could be assumed that a constant proportion of the stock of machinery is retired at each moment of time. Both assumptions tend
to ignore the problem of the evaluation of depreciation, insofar as
it depends on the age of the means of production.[13]

THE ACCUMULATION OF CAPITAL AND
THE ENTREPRENEURIAL CLASS

The foundation of the present model—similar in this respect to
almost every model since Adam Smith's time—is the general tendency of entrepreneurs to maximize their profits, as a necessary
condition of capitalistic development. Since entrepreneurs do not
consume and must invest all their income, an investment function
does not exist. The tendency towards maximum profit will always
correspond to the Marxian tendency towards maximum accumulation.

Given that the present model is free from an assumption of
competitive conditions, it may seem improper to put the profit
motive at the basis of the economic process. The growth of monopolistic enterprises may be based on other motives, such as the
maximization of sales.[14] These motives are, however, of less importance than the profit motive. They derive from the requirement
that enterprises also be concerned about "the things of this world"

[13] When technological discontinuities and technical progress are discussed
(see pp. 58 and 83), it will be shown that there are also reasons to believe
that changes in the age composition of machinery should not have permanent effects on the economy.

[14] Cf. W. J. Baumol, *Business Behavior, Value and Growth* (New York,
1959), chaps. vi–viii.

(e.g., political and social questions), and should be considered only as a specification of the maximum profit motive.[15]

The introduction of technical progress can be viewed as an increase in output per man (productivity) at constant total output.[16] Technical progress then frees labor in proportion to the increase in productivity. The quantity of this labor, by definition, equals the potential savings to entrepreneurs created by technical progress. Since these savings must be invested, the labor force freed by the new technique will be reabsorbed by means of an increase in the productive capacity of the system.[17]

The rate of accumulation is thus tightly linked to technical progress. Keeping population constant, the steady introduction of technical progress and the resulting rise in productivity, uniform in all sectors, corresponds to an increase in the labor force at the same rate at which productivity rises. The continuous introduction of technical progress, and the tendency towards maximum accumulation, have thus a fundamental role in ensuring that the system shall perpetuate itself in conditions of full employment and equilibrium. An additional condition, which will be described later, is that wage rates shall increase in proportion to the increase in productivity.

In the context of economic development, the literature has always given considerable weight to the possibility of a rate of accumulation insufficient to maintain full employment. In order to consider this possibility within my model, one of the assumptions must be changed and entrepreneurial consumption must be admitted. This question will be discussed at length below (see Chapter 5), but it may be useful to explain, at this point, one of the possible ways in which it could be dealt with.

---

[15] Cf. also H. T. Koplin, "The Profit Maximization Assumption," *Oxford Economic Papers* (July, 1963).

[16] For a more complete definition of technical progress, see Chapter 4 below.

[17] Chapter 5 will explain this process in detail. Mrs. Robinson gives considerable attention (in her *Accumulation of Capital*) to a rate of accumulation insufficient to maintain full employment, even though the assumption that entrepreneurs do not consume is not relaxed. She states that the existence of a potential surplus is not sufficient assurance that profits will be realized; according to her, for this to happen, it is necessary that investment be carried on, but it is not assured. Because entrepreneurs do not consume, and because she considers production processes which yield a surplus after paying the wage bill, Mrs. Robinson must assume that entrepreneurs "hoard" rather than invest, even in the long run. This assumption will be discussed below in some detail.

If entrepreneurs consume (in variable proportions) part of their profits and the assumption of a direct income-investment mechanism for entrepreneurs breaks down, under conditions of free competition no individual entrepreneur could guarantee the continuity of the system. He would not know that the introduction of a new, more productive technique unaccompanied by sufficient accumulation in the economy as a whole will create unemployment. Moreover, no individual entrepreneur would know how much investment would be needed to remedy such a disequilibrium.

If entrepreneurs were not able to assure a level of accumulation adequate to guarantee full employment, capitalist development would only be the result of chance, a clearly absurd conclusion. To avoid a complete anarchy of accumulation, we seem to have no course but to admit that entrepreneurs are conscious subjects of the economic process and act as a *class*. As soon as the class is introduced as a subject of economics in its own right, a series of difficult interpretative problems become relatively straightforward.

The means by which entrepreneurs constitute a non-heterogeneous group of interests is through a monopolistic structure of the market. The monopolist, or oligopolist, unlike the free-competition entrepreneur, is far enough above the market to observe the economy as a whole. In addition to their ability to influence prices and costs, monopolists can calculate, more or less approximately, the effects that the adoption of more productive techniques will have on the economy, particularly because these effects will also be felt by their enterprises. Thus monopolists know that decisions regarding their enterprises influence the economy as a whole, and that changes in the economy as a whole will in time also affect their enterprises. Monopolists cannot individually remedy, by altering their investment patterns and wage scales, a disequilibrium in the economy as a whole, even though they may be conscious of its existence. In this sense, monopolists and free-competition entrepreneurs are not very different. Where they do differ is in the capacity of the former to anticipate events which pertain to the economy as a whole. Therefore, if *all* monopolists are aware of a crisis that can damage each of them, it seems reasonable to assume that they will recognize themselves as a *class, or as a group of interests which becomes homogeneous at a macroeconomic level*. When a crisis strikes, monopolists will act in such a way as to influence the global quantities of wages, consumption, and profits.

The class becomes the "bridge" between micro- and macroeconomics.

The concept of a monopolistic class conscious of its economy-wide responsibilities is not introduced here as a *deus ex machina* to relieve the scholar of the necessity of studying behavioral patterns that would reconcile the actions of individual entrepreneurs with the needs of the economy: it is, rather, an attempt to introduce realism into the observation of capitalist society. Historians, I think, have demonstrated the conscious role played by economic groups or interests in the development of societies.

In conclusion, the anarchy of accumulation will be excluded from this model. It will be assumed that entrepreneurs know that a behavior which fails to provide sufficient accumulation for the economy creates a crisis that may endanger their own existence. It can be objected that, if the economy is in a state of continuous full employment, entrepreneurs' preferences will have to be subordinated to the demands of wage earners, since full employment reduces their bargaining power in setting wage rates. Marx felt that, in the long run, entrepreneurs would overcome this danger by adopting labor-saving techniques, thereby re-creating a "reserve army" of unemployed workers. As will be seen below, this argument is untenable: there will be a tendency to introduce the new labor-saving machinery in all sectors of the economy with resultant neutral, rather than labor-saving, technical progress (see pp. 81–82 below). Alternatively, Marx's argument can be interpreted as suggesting that accumulation will not be sufficient (cf. pp. 95–98 below), but this contrasts with the Marxian motive of maximum accumulation.

In this essay, it will be shown that entrepreneurs may allow the wage level to rise in presence of full employment (by means of a variety of policies, including non-economic ones) without a reduction of their bargaining power and without losing control of the system. All depends upon which class dictates conditions and which class accepts them.

ENTREPRENEURIAL EXPECTATIONS

The hypotheses made with regard to the rate of accumulation are closely related to those regarding the expectations of entrepreneurs. In the long period—an extended time period in which each historical event can be looked upon as a means toward, as well as a result of, the long-term goals of entrepreneurs—because entrepreneurs recognize themselves as a class, the dominant set of values will equal expectations. These expectations can well be frustrated, from time to time, by random happenings or technical difficulties. But these happenings and difficulties can always be taken as given; logically, they are unrelated to the expectations, and the set of aims will, somehow, discount them. Therefore, the structure of values, of expectations, and of results will not be affected. It is thus possible to eliminate those events and argue as though entrepreneurial expectations can always be realized.

This hypothesis of "omniscience" must be qualified and applied with care to the capitalist system. In fact, expectations of individual entrepreneurs at each moment of time can well be wrong and in conflict with each other. But it seems quite legitimate—because it is reasonable and, I think, proved by historical experience—to argue that every time an event is produced which can endanger the existence of the capitalist system, the entrepreneurial class is capable of taking measures sufficient to ensure its own stability. Through a variety of economic, political, and social instruments, the class controls its own future. Entrepreneurs are not "omnipotent" in addition to being "omniscient," but they do have the means correctly to foresee the future of economic activity, since they themselves are creating the reality they foresee.[18]

In conclusion, since we are dealing here with a long period of

[18] This hypothesis seems more realistic than those usually adopted in economic literature. In the neoclassical model, expectations are not important in the long run, since conditions of perfect competition are assumed, implying perfect foresight. For many modern economists expectations have, instead, a decisive role in the determination of the investment function. Mrs. Robinson, for example, assumes that at each moment entrepreneurs expect that the future rate of profits obtainable from an investment will continue indefinitely at the level prevailing in that moment (see *Accumulation of Capital*, p. 67). On the other hand, monopolists do not spontaneously limit their freedom in the choice of policies, and they certainly will not use only the policies of a freely competitive enterprise with the addition of partial control on quantities and prices. The economic system is not a direct democracy in which the participants always respect the rules of the game. Many economists, in accusing Marx of wrong forecasting, base their claims on the observation that the growth of capitalism (in the United States, in western Europe, in Japan) has been strong and quick; but if the actual system is taken as the basis of comparison for judging a theoretical model, it is only fair to avoid creating other theoretical models which are as far or farther from reality as is that of Marx. To paraphrase, "politics is the continuation of economics by other means." Without Roosevelt's social and political revolution, would the United States have overcome the Great Depression?

time, those entrepreneurial decisions which are subject to error lose importance, and only the decisions affecting the class as a whole are relevant. It is through these decisions, taken at discrete moments according to the circumstances and laws of the capitalist system, that the class corrects those errors which threaten to become cumulative.

CYCLICAL FLUCTUATIONS AND THE LONG-RUN TREND

This hypothesis of entrepreneurial class consciousness may clarify the problem of the relationship between business cycles and trend. It has been said that fluctuations originate from errors in entrepreneurial expectations. For example, when entrepreneurs foresee an increase of output and augment productive capacity correspondingly, they "have a tendency to behave as though they expected the consequent high level of profit to be maintained in the future,"[19] but since productive capacity continues to increase as a result of these expectations, the rate of profits will eventually decline. A series of fluctuations is thus created within the economy. But if entrepreneurial expectations produce the phenomenon of fluctuations, they cannot simultaneously be responsible for the long-run trend of the economy. This dilemma has worried economists, and many attempts have been made to explain either the fluctuations or the trend.[20] However, no satisfactory explanation of both phenomena has been proposed. Pasinetti has described the difficulty as follows: "macroeconomic models which dictate a regular fluctuating pattern to economic activity cannot explain economic growth, and . . . theories which can define or can base themselves

[19] Robinson, "The Model of an Expanding Economy," in *Collected Economic Papers*.

[20] The literature on this subject is very extensive. Omitting those contributions which, in dealing with growth problems, also deal with business cycles, it will be sufficient to cite a few studies on the specific problem of the relationship between cycle and trend: J. Steindl, *Maturity and Stagnation in American Capitalism* (Oxford, 1952), chap. xiii; R. M. Goodwin, "The Problem of Trend and Cycle," *Yorkshire Bulletin of Economic and Social Research* (August, 1953); N. Kaldor, "The Relation of Economic Growth and Cyclical Fluctuation," in E. Lundberg (ed.), *The Business Cycle in the Postwar Period* (London, 1955); A. Smithies, "Economic Fluctuations and Growth," *Econometrica* (January, 1957); L. Pasinetti, "Fluttuazioni cicliche e sviluppo economico," *L'Industria* (January–March, 1960); R. C. O. Matthews, *The Trade Cycle* (Cambridge, 1959), chap. xiii.

on conditions of dynamic equilibrium are not able to explain fluctu-ations."[21]

The problem depends, to a large extent, on the assumptions in-cluded in interpretative models. Even though cyclical fluctuations will not play a role in these pages, above all because they are a short-term phenomenon, the hypotheses made with regard to entrepreneurial expectations seem capable of reconciling—at least conceptually—the phenomena of cycles and trend. Expectations of entrepreneurs, seen individually and in the short term, always produce fluctuations, which are related not only to the random events already mentioned but, more particularly, to the entrepre-neurial tendency to outstrip real movements in economic quantities. Because of the class apparatus of capitalism, these fluctuations are never so serious as to endanger the existence of the system. At the same time, the class consciousness of entrepreneurs and the rise of subsistence consumption ensure a growth trend to the economy. This is, of course, not an elegant explanation because it does not rely on any self-correcting feature of business expectations, but on direct and discrete interventions of the entrepreneurial class.

MARKET STRUCTURE, ENTERPRISES, INDUSTRIES

The present model is clearly not one of perfect competition. Not only is the prevalent market structure monopolistic, but specific groups can intervene as an equilibrium factor. In the context of this analysis, it is not necessary to specify a particular market form. The notion of monopoly, therefore, includes any market structure other than that of perfect competition.

The enterprises which form the productive system are not neces-sarily defined by the commodities they produce. Each enterprise may produce a number of commodities and may vary the composi-tion of its output without constraints. On the other hand, I shall maintain, for as long as it proves useful, the distinction between the sector producing investment goods and the sector producing consumer goods. Industries are defined by the commodity they produce. The phenomenon of product differentiation, although not easily differentiated from the notion of new products, will not be taken into account, principally because it is likely to be valid only

[21] "Fluttuazioni cicliche," pp. 20–21.

in the Marshallian short period.[22] We deal with the enterprise, as it has been defined, in touching on the subject of the life span of monopolistic entities, and with the industry, as it has been defined, in speaking of the structure of profit rates in the economy.

THE MEASURE

The problem of measuring economic quantities has not been faced thus far. It arises, however, as soon as the composition of consumption is allowed to change and new products are allowed on the market. Since a change in the composition of total output (and of investment) must accompany a change in the composition of consumption, and since it is not possible to measure directly a particular mix of commodities in terms of another mix, when both are composed of different commodities or of the same commodities in different proportions,[23] many of the hypotheses elaborated above may seem to lose their validity. For example, any definition of a new production technique (at an aggregate level) which is clearly preferable to a technique previously in use must be conducted with reference to the output resulting from both techniques. However, such a definition would lose its meaning if the composition of the output from one technique were different from that of the other. Similarly, if both techniques and composition of output change, the composition of investment will also change, and all inter-temporal comparisons of investment flows become impossible.

Even though it is the most important single concept in these pages, the rate of profits is also difficult to define, once the intuitive notion is discarded. In a system in which wages equal the subsistence level of income, profits are a residue depending for their magnitude on the production technique. Insofar as wages are higher than the subsistence level of income, profits are set by the forces determining income distribution. However, when the com-

---

[22] Product differentiation should not be relevant in the long run, since it is unrelated to changes in consumption. The classical exposition of this phenomenon is E. H. Chamberlin's *The Theory of Monopolistic Competition* (Cambridge, Mass., 1948), chap. iv. Product differentiation is considered by this author as a cause of monopolistic market forms. It seems to me, however, that product differentiation can only arise when certain essential characteristics of a perfect competition market are already absent (e.g., the independence of demand from supply, the "atomism" of supply).

[23] For a clear exposition of this problem, see K. E. Boulding, *A Reconstruction of Economics* (New York, 1950), chaps. x and xi.

position of output is changed, the composition of profits in terms of commodities will change, and the problem of the measurement of profits arises, unless a totally unrealistic assumption of the perfect interchangeability of commodities, in a physical sense, is introduced. Similarly, the notion of invested capital on which profits are measured is also obscure, as was already pointed out.[24] Moreover, it will be shown that there exists a plurality of profit rates and that the profit rate for the economy as a whole is difficult to determine. To all these difficulties, I shall not add that deriving from the correspondence between the rate of profits and the rate of interest. The model will be in real terms, as far as possible, and the monetary aspects will be disregarded.

It is not my purpose to isolate the problem of measuring capital from that of measuring all values. The difficulties encountered in considering the relationship between wage rates and rates of profits for the purposes of measuring capital are overwhelming and largely meaningless. Any study of these relationships undertaken solely for that purpose contributes little to the identification of the deeper causes of the variation in the rates of wages and of profits.

This research will conclude (see p. 138 below) that the measurement problem as faced in the economic literature from Ricardo to Walras to Sraffa—as a search, that is, for an unchanging measure of value capable of furnishing meaningful quantitative results—cannot be solved. This impossibility should not represent an unsurmountable obstacle to the further development of economic theory (unlike Heisenberg's "indetermination" principle, which seems to have impeded the theoretical development of physics). In my model, which admits a rationalizing principle in the class consciousness of entrepreneurs, there exists a simple, logical solution, which, if it does not provide a measure in quantitative terms, does permit the analysis of the capitalist system. Even though much less elegant that Ricardo's, Walras', or Sraffa's measures, the terms of reference adopted here can be utilized for a generalized interpretation.

Historical experience shows that in economic reality there has always been a dynamism in social preferences. Even if it cannot be measured directly, a notion of *increase* in output and income, although their composition may change, is always present in society.

---

[24] In addition to those elements already mentioned, the value of invested capital logically includes the element of profit (and/or interest).

This notion, in fact, has a direct relationship to the change in the composition of consumption and is of the same nature as the concept used to explain the rise in the psychological subsistence level of income. If the universal conscience identified in changes in composition an increase in output and in income, it would suffice for engaging in logical comparisons of different techniques of production in terms of their output, and for measuring the dimensions of a system through time. This postulate implies that it is necessary to use a value judgment of an historical-social type in order to analyze the long-term tendency of an economic system.

There is no doubt that the value judgment defined here is another *a posteriori* measure, which depends upon the play of other economic factors. But it will be possible to show that such judgment is not only, or not particularly, a *result* of economic activity, but more surely a reflection of the preferences and of the complex of aims of the entrepreneurial class. As such, that value judgment becomes an *a priori* measure. The class permeates with its own aims all the vast complex of social values which, reinterpreted in the preferences expressed by the community, represents a logical, systematic measure of the output of the economy. This measure will be unchanging insofar as its content—the complex of aims of the class—is also unchanging. It will be necessary to postulate such constancy because an examination in detail of the aims of the entrepreneurial class is outside the scope of economics. As a result of this assumption, it will be possible to say that the development of relative prices as time goes on does not imperil the equilibrium of the system. It will not be possible, on the other hand, to reconstruct the system of entrepreneurial preferences in order to extract a measure for quantitative analyses, given the variability of development factors through time. It will only be possible to say that such a preference system exists.

Economists will not like this unfamiliar and descriptive yardstick, while philosophers, although happy to see some logic infiltrating our science, will no doubt object to its shallowness. I cannot help the philosophers. The economists, however, may find comfort in the thought that economics, even without possessing any serious measure of value, has made considerable progress, probably as a result of the presence in each economist's mind of a value judgment of the kind described above. Without such a postulate no non-economist could understand what economics is all about.

The logical measure suggested here is necessary in order to pass from a microeconomic analysis to one of the economy as a whole, and in order to give meaning to long-period studies. There is nothing wrong, however, in establishing comparisons and in selecting techniques according to their productivity when the commodity mix produced by each technique is constant. It is mainly at the level of the economy as a whole that the measure defined above becomes relevant.

In studying technical progress and in discussing the rate of accumulation (or the increase in the system's productive capacity), it will be necessary to maintain the assumption that the composition of output remains unchanged. A comparison of techniques, even though logically possible, would hardly be understandable without such an assumption.

If the measure advanced here is acceptable, if technical progress is uniformly distributed among the different sectors of the economy, if capital accumulation is always sufficient to maintain full employment, and if wages rise in proportion to productivity, it is possible to observe an economic system in equilibrium, in which the rate of profits is given and constant. In equilibrium, the concept of capital is clear and becomes a logical category dependent upon other mechanisms operating in the economy. The value of capital, measured in terms of hours of labor, calculated at the given rate of profits, multiplied by the real wage equals the value of capital in terms of commodities.[25] Both aspects of the value of capital have a definite meaning, and capital becomes an aggregable concept. The production function, however, remains a useless concept because it would now be constructed by taking as given the rate of profits —and therefore could not determine it—and because I will show that it does not even exist as a schedule of alternative technical possibilities.

All this suggests that, while the problem of measuring capital is not really autonomous nor solvable when seen in isolation, the interpretation of economic development depends on the measurability of output. Since the measure used here is only "logical" in nature, it cannot be utilized from outside the frame of reference to which it pertains (the class). An independent observer cannot, therefore, use it as a quantitative yardstick. More of this question later. At this point it is perhaps useful to indicate that, as a consequence, it is not possible to picture an equilibrium system *from the*

[25] This is Mrs. Robinson's conclusion in *Accumulation of Capital*.

start; it is only possible to reconstruct one after examining the forces that tend to maintain it.

THE NOTION OF EQUILIBRIUM

The preceding analysis hinted at one conclusion which will be more evident later: the capitalist system, even within the restrictive assumptions on which the present model is based, does not possess mechanical features that can maintain it in equilibrium. However, at least within the present non-dialectical analysis, it can be shown that the system is capable of overcoming its many contradictions[26] and of reproducing itself, and that this capability depends largely on the self-awareness of the entrepreneurial class. Equilibrium thus has in these pages a historical rather than a truly economic meaning, which may be the only possible meaning over a period of time as long as that described here. In this respect, the procedure is not far from that of Marx.

CONCLUSION

It has been necessary to spend considerable time defining hypotheses, postulates, and assumptions in order to free the analysis from many awkward peculiarities and to build a simple model that would still be useful for an exercise in interpretation. It is now possible to examine in detail the principal conditions of the working of the model. I believe that the model has succeeded in identifying certain structural characteristics of the capitalist system which may not have been properly evaluated in the past. An analysis of the relationships between these characteristics and the growth of the system is possible, even in the presence of the measurement problem.

---

[26] Since this analysis is far from being complete, one cannot also conclude that capitalism will last forever. The simple fact that it has been replaced by other economic forms in certain countries shows that contradictions must be inherent in its social-economic nature.

3

A STRUCTURAL ASPECT OF ECONOMIC GROWTH: THE DIFFERENTIATION OF PROFIT RATES

In this chapter the increase in subsistence wages in the long run will be considered as given. The analysis, thus, begins with an economic system in which consumption—which equals workers' income—increases with time. As incomes grow, the composition of the economy's output changes. Many authors have discussed the case of a variation in the composition of output originating from the competing claims on resources of the sectors producing investment goods and consumer goods. In allocating resources between these two sectors, a judgment is also passed on the composition of the resulting output, and many observations can be made as to the latter's influence on the growth process. Although this is certainly an important problem, it will be excluded from the present model (however, it will be discussed briefly later). In any case, this particular change in the composition of output is not the only one that occurs in the growth process. Perhaps more relevant is the variation in the composition of output resulting from the variation in the composition of consumption.

ENGEL'S LAW

That the composition of consumption changes as income increases is not a new observation. Engel[1] was the first to notice the phenomenon. One of his empirical studies showed that expenditure on food, as a share of total consumer expenditure, is, on the average, a decreasing function of income.[2]

It is easy to generalize this law. Consumers, after they have satisfied primary needs, however they are defined, can, with a rise in income, satisfy non-essential needs or, at least, needs which are less essential than the primary ones. Thus consumption of commodities which satisfy less essential needs will increase more

[1] Cf. J. A. Schumpeter, *History*, p. 961.
[2] Of course, if Engel's law depends upon the increase in income (available for consumption), the pace at which income increases should influence the shape of the function expressing Engel's law. This problem has not been studied here.

rapidly than consumption of commodities satisfying primary needs. Engel's law is an expression of the fundamental postulate of economic science—the foundation of the principle of decreasing marginal utility—that needs and commodities can be classified by degree of "importance" (utility, preference, etc.). Engel's law, therefore, works independent of the price system or, to put it more clearly, it determines or contributes toward determining the dynamics of the price system in the long run.

In fact, if the economic system were in "natural" equilibrium, Engel's law would become a true *law of value*. However, it will be shown that the equilibrium of the system is not ensured by endogenous, "natural" mechanisms. Thus there is a problem of reconciliation of Engel's law on the one hand and all those forces which make for the equilibrium of the capitalist system on the other.

In a diagram showing a system of indifference curves for each consumer, Engel's law can be expressed as a curve linking all positions of equilibrium of the consumer budget with the change of income. This curve, variously called "Engel's curve" or "curve of consumed income" or "living standard curve," is valid only *a posteriori*, since it is traced at given prices.

Analysis of Engel's law has been limited almost exclusively to studies in applied economics, where the problem is one of determining the existence of a saturation level of consumption under conditions of rising income for an individual commodity or group of commodities present in consumer budgets. It is not our purpose to delve into the problems raised by these studies, but it may be useful to quote a few of them[3] because they confirm the validity of Engel's law not only for each consumer but also for the economy as a whole. It is surprising that Engel's law has found so little application in economy-wide theoretical models.[4] Perhaps this is the

[3] The list is long, and what follows only illustrates the kind of studies undertaken in this field: R. G. D. Allen and A. L. Bowley, *Family Expenditure* (London, 1935); J. Aitchison and J. A. C. Brown, "A Synthesis of Engel Curve Theory," *Review of Economic Studies* (1953–54); H. S. Houthakker, "La forme des courbes d'Engel," *Cahiers Seminaire Econometrie*, No. 2 (1954); S. G. Prais, "Non-Linear Estimates of Engel Curves," *Review of Economic Studies* (December, 1954); Prais and Houthakker, *The Analysis of Family Budgets* (Cambridge, 1955); Houthakker, "An International Comparison of Household Expenditure Patterns," *Econometrica* (October, 1957).

[4] Schumpeter (*History*, p. 961) has written: "Neither Engel himself nor anyone else seems to have realized [the law's] interest for economic *theory*." G. del Vecchio, however, studied the subject as early as 1922 ("Relazioni tra

result of the macroeconomic treatment to which consumption has been subjected in economic analysis.

The phenomenon described in Engel's law occurs continually in a growing economy. I consider it to be a long-period phenomenon. When viewed in a macroeconomic context, Engel's law is only a manifestation of the variability of the subsistence level of consumption. Only after having satisfied primary needs does one satisfy secondary needs, and when this behavior is repeated a number of times, it becomes evident that what were in the past secondary needs have become in the present primary ones, in comparison with other needs which were further down in the consumer's scale of priority in the past. It is precisely the gradual absorption of a number of commodities in the subsistence level of consumption that makes Engel's law operative.

THE TREND IN CONSUMPTION AND DISTRIBUTION OF INVESTMENT

A natural consequence of this asymmetry in the growth process is that industries producing commodities the consumption of which increases more rapidly than that of commodities produced by other industries must expand most rapidly. Abstracting for the moment from the change in technical conditions of production, what is the effect of differing output growth rates on investment levels? If the incremental capital-output ratio in the fast-growing industry is equal to or higher than the ratio in the slow-growing industry, then investment will be larger in the former (in absolute terms) than in the latter. When, however, the incremental capital-output ratio in the fast-growing industry is lower than the ratio in the slow-growing industry, then investment in the former may not be larger *in absolute terms* than investment in the latter. If the latter does not grow at all, there is no problem: its net investment is zero. But

entrata e consumo," *Giornale degli economisti e annali di economia*, pp. 111–42, 223–51). L. Spaventa has recently analyzed critically some of the problems relating to the introduction of Engel's law in a growth model ("Effetti di variazioni strutturali nella composizione della domanda sulla produttività del lavoro e sull'occupazione," in Spaventa [ed.], *Nuovi problemi di sviluppo economico* [Turin, 1962]). A. Pedone, in the same volume ("Appunti sull'introduzione della domanda in un modello generale di produzione"), writes: "One can take into account an increase in demand . . . which is not uniformly distributed among different sectors only if the uniformity of the rate of profit of the system is abandoned" (p. 255), which is the thesis of this essay. Pedone's conclusions and mine have been developed independently.

if it grows, then the capital-output ratio plays a role. On the other hand, whatever this role, the fast-growing industry will always show a *relatively* higher level of investment than the slow-growing industry. In fact, the ratio of the investment needed in the fast-growing industry to the investment needed in the slow-growing industry would be *higher* than it would be if the former also had to grow at the slower rate of the latter.[5]

Therefore, given the incremental capital-output ratios, individual industries can be classified, in relation to their respective investment levels, according to the rate of increase of consumption of the commodities produced by each of them. Since fast-growing industries must attract—or create within themselves—a larger amount of means of production (in absolute or relative terms) than industries which grow more slowly,[6] *the profit rates shown by the first group of industries must be higher than the profit rates shown by the second.*

AN EXAMPLE: TWO INDUSTRIES

This section will illustrate, in a very simplified fashion, the reasons for considering the differentiated structure of profit rates as a permanent characteristic of the economy.

I will disregard, for the moment, the general model described above, and deal only with a particular situation. The hypotheses which were used to build the general model need not now be taken into account, at least insofar as they are only useful in that model.

Let us also abstract here from the matrix of interindustrial relationships and observe only two industries producing consumer goods: industry I, producing commodity *i*, and industry A, producing commodity *a*.[7] Since I shall speak of the means of production in both industries, it would seem necessary to add at least one more industry, which supplies the means of production to both A and I. However, the argument that follows holds also if we take

---

[5] In symbols, for industry A, $I_a = \alpha DP_a$, in which I_a = investment, P_a = output, and α = the incremental capital output ratio; for industry B, $I_b = \beta DP_b$. If $\alpha = \beta$, and if $DP_a/P_a > DP_b/P_b$, then $I_a > I_b$ and, *a fortiori*, if $\alpha > \beta$. If, instead, $\alpha < \beta$, I_a/I_b (when $DP_a/P_a > DP_b/P_b$) $> I_a/I_b$ (when $DP_a/P_a = DP_b/P_b$).

[6] The assumption here is, of course, that there is competition over the resources available for investment.

[7] If the reader prefers the flavor of the real, he can read "industry" for I and "agriculture" for A, even though these associations are obviously inaccurate.

only two industries, provided that each industry supplies means of production to the other industry in addition to its production for final consumption.[8]

Let us suppose that consumption of both *i* and *a* is constant at a certain level for an initial period and that, after the initial period, consumption of commodity *i* grows at a given rate. In order to further simplify this illustration, let us suppose that consumption of *a* declines symmetrically with the increase of consumption of *i*— in other words, it declines at the rate at which the consumption of *i* grows. Let us also suppose that in the initial period, when consumption of both commodities is constant, the rates of profits of industry I and of industry A are equal (were they different, but constant, the argument would not be affected).

Let us imagine that entrepreneurs in I and A are taken by surprise[9] at the sudden divergence in consumption trends of commodities *a* and *i* and that, in both I and A, production will continue for some time at the level prevailing in the preceding period. This implies that commodity *a* is being produced in quantities exceeding demand, while commodity *i* is being produced in quantities insufficient to satisfy demand. Let us look at industry A. Since there is excess production in relation to consumption, the price of *a* will decline;[10] and since the level of production has not changed, the rate of profits will decline. Conversely, in industry I the price of *i* and the rate of profits will increase.[11]

---

[8] For the hypothesis of different rates of growth to be valid, it is sufficient for industry I not to absorb all the output of industry A (or vice versa). All this will become clearer below, pp. 60–61.

[9] This hypothesis of qualified "omniscience" is applicable only to those cases of possible disequilibria which are relevant for the class as a whole. As was already indicated, there is nothing to prevent the expectations of individual entrepreneurs from being wrong.

[10] Whatever the market form, the price will have to decline because of fear of a further decrease in consumption; whatever the shape of cost curves, the profit rate will also decline. Also, whatever the supply elasticities, the profit rate cannot be maintained in the face of a reduction of sales unless production techniques are changed. On this, see below, pp. 51, 58, and Chapter 5.

[11] The question of how much prices of *a* and *i* must change in order to create a certain differential in profit rates is not studied in this essay. The reader can imagine that price changes and changes in profit rates are symmetrical in both industries. But, in general, this assumption is not realistic: there is no reason why prices in *a* and in *i* should change in proportion to the change in the rates of profits. First, the differential in the rates of profits which induces movements in means of production may be different in different industries, in relation to the "stickiness" of each industry vis-à-vis the capital market. Second, the increase in price of commodity *i*, necessary to

Let us assume that means of production are freely interchangeable among sectors. As soon as a differential between profit rates in two industries is formed, the means of production will tend to move from the industry which offers a lower rate of profits toward the industry which offers a higher one. The means of production will thus shift from A to I. This movement permits an increase of production in I and a decrease of production in A and continues until the profit rates in both industries are equal. This situation occurs as soon as industry I has increased its productive capacity so as to satisfy fully the consumption of *i* and, conversely, as soon as industry A has decreased its productive capacity so as to exactly satisfy the (reduced) consumption of *a*.

If consumption trends for both commodities were equal from this point onward, then the profit rate of the system would remain uniform; no further movement in means of production would be needed. However, because consumption trends for *a* and *i*, in the long run, are different, the movements observed above will be continually repeated, and a differential between the profit rate of *a* and that of *i* will be continually created and reabsorbed.

If these movements are repeated a number of times, it is possible to observe that in industry I there exists an upper level of the profit rate which corresponds to each variation of the production level of I; similarly, in industry A there exists a lower level of the profit rate. In both I and A, there is also a lower and an upper level, respectively. The two levels of profit rates in I, as well as in A, are not symmetrical from a heuristic point of view. The higher level in

---

increase the rate of profits in industry I by a certain amount, depends also on the quantity of other factors used in the production of *i*. For example:

	Commodity *i*		Commodity *a*	
	Time 0	Time 1	Time 0	Time 1
Unit price	20	25	50	45
Cost of factor X	10	10	40	40
Cost of capital	10	15	10	5
Invested capital	100	100	100	100
Rate of profit	10%	15%	10%	5%
Change in the rate of profit		+50%		−50%
Change in price		+25%		−10%

This example is proposed only in order to show the arithmetical properties of changes in prices and changes in profit rates. It is not an illustration of the argument presented in the text.

I permits an increase in productive capacity, while the lower level arrests this increase as it reaches the level needed to satisfy consumption. When consumption increases continually, it is obvious that the profit rate will tend to be at or near the higher level. Therefore, the *normal* level of the profit rate in I is the upper one, since it is the one which allows a steady increase in productive capacity to match the steady increase in consumption. Conversely, the *normal* level of the profit rate in A is the lower one.

The lower level of the profit rate in I is valid only in the short run and is caused, in the first place, by the time required to adjust production levels. In the example given, the lower profit rate is also due to the entrepreneur's mistake, insofar as he does not foresee that productive capacity will have to increase anew, and this error in turn depends on his inability to foresee that consumption of commodity *i* will increase continuously. I shall comment again below on this "mistake."

The rationale for the creation of a differential in profit rates is understandable enough: if consumption behaves as dictated by Engel's law, it is only through the creation of such a differential that the means of production can flow continuously into I and out of A. We could also assume, without meeting serious logical obstacles, that the means of production are rigidly fixed, so that any movement of the means of production between A and I would concern new investment exclusively. In the real world this is the norm, since the trends in consumption of *a* and *i* which have been described should rather be viewed as trends in the growth rates of consumption (see below).

The example has been based on a "deficit" forecast of consumption levels on the part of entrepreneurs in I and of a "surplus" forecast in A. What happens if expectations are reversed, to a "deficit" in A and a "surplus" in I? Not very much. It is clear that if the output of *i* grows faster than its consumption—and with the consequent decrease in price, the rate of profits declines—in a previous moment there must have been an investment in I sufficient to create the capacity for the production which is now running ahead of consumption. This investment must have taken place through a movement of resources from A to I and through the creation of a differential between profit rates. Thus, this case is not different from the previous one. The process of differentiation of profit rates will repeat itself, and an upper and lower level of the rate of profit in I and in A will be created.

QUALIFICATIONS

It is now necessary to qualify the validity of the example and the results obtained by it. To begin with, the example dealt with both an increase in the consumption of i and a decrease in the consumption of a. A more realistic case, and in line with Engel's law, is that of an increase in the percentage of total consumption satisfied by i or a decrease in the percentage satisfied by a. Therefore, a decrease in the consumption of a does not imply an absolute decline (in other words, a decrease in the rate of growth of consumption). This does not affect the example, but does show that the movement of the means of production, induced by differential profit rates, is related to new investment and shares in new investment of each sector, rather than to movements in the existing capital stock.

Is it possible to argue that each time the rate of profits in I tends towards its lower level, the over-all rate of profits in fact tends toward uniformity? Not really; the profit rate can never tend toward uniformity as an equilibrium position—not even potentially—since we are not talking of a stationary universe but of a universe where the relative importance of each sector changes continuously.

It is worth emphasizing that the differentiation process is valid in the long run. It depends on the changes in the composition of consumption, which, in turn, are a function of the changes in the psychological subsistence level of consumption.

The differentiation of profit rates (the upper level for I, the lower level for A) does not depend upon assumptions relating to entrepreneurial expectations. In the example given above, when entrepreneurs make mistakes the differentiation takes place. But even if individual entrepreneurs foresee the future correctly, the divergence in profit rates would not disappear. Since each industry must continuously attract means of production at a faster rate than other industries, profit rates must be different. In other words, when entrepreneurs correctly foresee the future, the movement in prices and resources, which is the basis of the process of divergence in profit rates, is discounted beforehand by entrepreneurs in I and A. Profit rates in I and A do not ever need to become equal again.

I have not yet considered the role of changing techniques of production in the rise or decline of the rate of growth of output in the two industries. As will be shown later, since full employment conditions prevail, new techniques will be introduced all the time.[12] It may well happen that the new techniques show different productivity in the two sectors or, in other words, that changes in techniques in both sectors will not maintain constant their productivity ratio. In this case, all relevant ratios of both industries, as well as the conditions under which the differentiation of profit rates occurs, would change. The prices of commodities *a* and *i* would be subject to a variation independent of that which gives rise to the differentiation of profit rates. To avoid this difficulty, it was implicitly assumed above that the change in techniques would have a neutral effect on the ratio of the two sectors' productivities. The question cannot be pursued further at this stage of our analysis, since we are not yet looking at the economy as a whole but only at relationships between particular sectors. It can be argued provisionally, however, that even if an industry were to adopt new techniques the productivity of which, in relation to the productivity of those in another sector, is different from that of the old techniques, the divergence of profit rates may well be affected in degree but would not be affected *in principle*; it would still depend upon relative consumption trends, which are independent from the variations in the productivity ratios.

The profit differentiation mechanism, at least at this preliminary stage, is neutral in relation to the long-run trend of the *general* rate of profits of the economy (or the "average" rate, or the range of values covered by the family of profit rates in the economy); in other words, we are considering changes within the framework of a general profit rate. However, the obscure nature of the concept of profit rate for the economy as a whole is certainly not clarified by the differentiation mechanism. Even if the range of profit rates covered by the different industrial profit rates, rather than a general rate of profit, is considered, the haziness of the concept is not dispelled. The movements of such rates may be so frequent that observation of the range itself becomes difficult. There is no choice, on the other hand, but to assume that the movements of the range —or of the "average" profit rate—can be identified.

Figures 1, 2, and 3 illustrate the example. They do not indicate any precise quantitative relationships. In the three figures the horizontal axis represents time and the vertical axis the share of total

[12] The necessity of accepting this hypothesis is illustrated below in Chapter 5, pp. 93–95, 103–5.

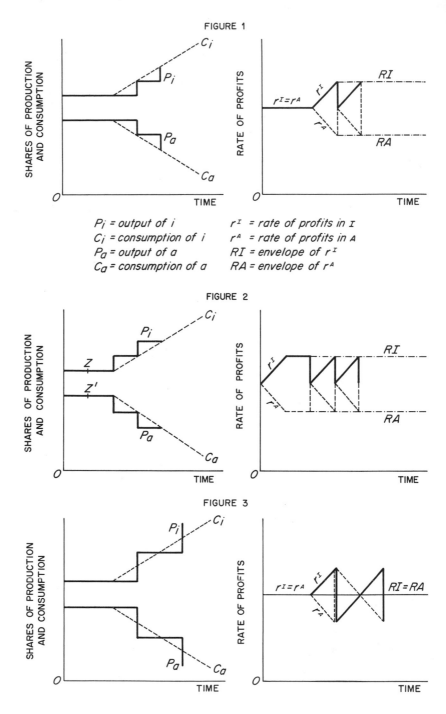

FIGURE 1

P_i = output of i r^I = rate of profits in I
C_i = consumption of i r^A = rate of profits in A
P_a = output of a RI = envelope of r^I
C_a = consumption of a RA = envelope of r^A

FIGURE 2

FIGURE 3

quantities consumed and produced, as well as the rate of profits in both industries. *RI* shows the long-term trend of the rate of profits in I. Figure 2 shows the case of a "surplus" forecast in I. *Z* designates the moment in time at which entrepreneurs in I must have invested to produce the quantities expected for the future. Figure 3 shows, within the framework of our example, the case normally described in the economic literature. Profit rates in I and A show regular fluctuations around an average level representing the uniform rate of profit. It is only with a behavior of this kind that profit rates can be said to tend towards uniformity. On the other hand, such behavior is absurd because it would imply that the means of production continue to move from A to I (or vice versa) even after profit rates have reached equality.[13]

THE ROLE OF MONOPOLIES

At this point, an apparent contradiction arises between, on the one hand, the permanent differentiation of profit rates, or the fact that certain industries will have to be content with a rate of profit on invested capital that is lower than the rate obtained in other industries, and, on the other hand, the fundamental motive of capitalist development, namely, the effort of all entrepreneurs toward maximum profit rates. A reconciliation of this contradiction can be found as soon as market forms other than those of perfect competition are introduced. Monopolistic structures tend to isolate different industries so as to make possible the simultaneous presence of different profit rates. Monopolistic forms are sometimes presented in the economic literature more as a result of psychological tendencies originating from man's nature (*à la* Hobbes) than as a structural element of the capitalist system. Almost invariably, however, the literature has considered monopolistic market forms as random changes in competitive conditions determined by the confused status of the real as opposed to the abstract. In fact, very few economists outside the Marxian school have tried to determine which market form is consistent with the economic system they are describing.

In this analysis, monopolistic market forms are the nature of the

[13] Given the lack of discussion on this whole subject, it is not surprising that there are so few statistical analyses which can show the principal characteristics of the differentiation of profit rates. A recent empirical investigation, however, has done a valuable pioneering job: G. J. Stigler, *Capital and Rates of Return in Manufacturing Industries* (Princeton, N.J., 1963), especially chap. iv.

system. They are the only means by which it is possible to distinguish the rates of profits obtained by different industries and to assure the growth of different industries in step with the consumption trend confronting each of them. Looked at in this way, monopolistic market forms are permanent features of capitalism. Perfect competition and monopolistic forms cannot therefore be analyzed as equally good approximations to reality. It will be the entrepreneurial class itself—which I have defined as self-aware only when composed of monopolists or quasi-monopolists—that provides social, legal, and political protection for monopolistic structures.

Once the monopolistic scene is viewed thus, it also becomes clear that it is unnecessary for the economy to show a progressive rise in the degree of concentration.[14] The structure of consumption and its trend ensure the continuous existence of industries the consumption of whose product increases at a lower rate than the consumption of the products of other industries. As a result, even though the *industrial* composition of monopolistic forms may change in the long run, the monopolistic structure itself need not change.

It is important to stress that, for the argument to hold, it is only necessary that one part of production be monopolistic: that which includes the industries with high profit rates. The industries which show lower profit rates do not need to be as closed or as monopolistic as the others. One could push this point further and state that the prevalent market form in one industry depends on the consumption trends of the commodities produced by that industry relative to the consumption trends confronted by other industries. Those industries for which consumption rises at a faster rate will be more monopolistic (more concentrated) than others.

THE FINANCIAL MARKET AND SELF-FINANCING

The difference between the profit rates of two industries is maintained by the process of transfer of the means of production from one industry to the other. But the free circulation of capital is not easily reconcilable with the existence of monopolistic market forms. This is a problem that can be solved.

---

[14] This observation is necessary because it has not been fully proved that, in the long run, the degree of concentration increases. The problem, once again, is to find the measure with which to compare degrees of concentration in time.

First, it is possible that the movement of capital may be in one direction only: from the industries confronting "dying" consumption to the industries facing rapidly growing consumption. Since only the latter need to be more concentrated, it will not be difficult for means of production to flow inward. It will be difficult for them to flow outward, and this reinforces the monopolistic character of the more dynamic enterprises. As the structure of consumption changes and the consumption of certain commodities starts to increase rapidly, the industries producing these commodities will become more monopolistic and will require and obtain more means of production. The industries that were highly monopolistic at an earlier stage will become less so and will release capital to the faster growing ones. As a result, there is no need for a "free" circulation of capital, but only for a one-way movement. Second, it has been pointed out that the movement of resources consisted not so much of means of production already in use, but of new means of production being created in the different industries of the economy. Now, the existence of monopolies in the "physical" production market does not necessarily imply the same monopolistic structure in the financial market. The individuals who control the former do not necessarily control the latter. On the other hand, the stronger the monopolist, and the easier his recourse to the financial market is, the lower the price differential needed to build up resources for the more dynamic (more monopolistic) industry will be. This observation reveals an interesting "propaganda" feature of the system: the monopolistic price effect will be less if the monopolist is strong and can tap the financial market easily. Although the relative price situation will not be different when expressed in real terms, the monopolists' effect on prices in the real world will not seem as monopolistic as it really is. This "propaganda" effect of the financial market is not very important quantitatively, since it is self-defeating. The ease with which an industry taps the capital market depends upon its monopolistic strength, and this strength would be adversely affected if the industry began to set prices as though there were free competition. As a result, prices will remain "sticky" —perhaps a shade less than they would be without a capital market to tap—and the industry's recourse to the financial market will be less frequent than its monopolistic status would suggest. Weaker industries will thus become active on the financial market. What appears as the "free" circulation of capital is therefore not obstructed by the monopolistic market structure and by profit rate differentiation. Self-financing of the stronger industries becomes the way in which new means of production to match the trend in consumption are acquired. The monopolistic character of industries producing for a dynamic consumption helps self-financing, and self-financing helps the growth of these industries. The greater the growth potential of an industry (or of an enterprise) in relation to the growth rate of the consumption of the commodity it produces, the larger the quantity of new means of production obtained by that industry and utilized by it will be.[15]

THE ORIGIN OF MONOPOLIES

The statement that the differentiation of profit rates justifies the existence of monopolistic market forms in the capitalist system is not clearly demonstrable. Such statements are difficult to prove conclusively, since economics is a science which cannot re-create in the laboratory the processes it describes. It is, however, necessary to see whether or not other reasons for the formation of monopolies exist which can be made part of the pattern of capitalist growth and which will stand up as well as or better than the explanation proposed above, in which monopolies are seen to originate from the laws of the development of consumption and the differentiation of profit rates. The economic literature has always considered the differentiation of profit rates as a direct result of the existence of monopolistic market forms, rather than the other way around. An examination of reality itself shows the existence of a variety of monopolistic forms and of profit rates: a large number of empirical studies have confirmed the popular notion. Neoclassical economists have interpreted these phenomena as short-term variations which do not in the long run disturb the equilibrium of a perfect competition market where there is a uniform profit rate, or profit rates tending towards uniformity.[16] The three-decade discussion of market forms has already proved, however, that the capitalist system is incompatible with conditions of perfect competition. P. Sraffa[17] was the first to show that the demand for a commodity is not really

---

[15] This does not imply that capitalism gives rise to rigid structures which, once established, must continue to grow. If this were so, capitalism could become contradictory, since the composition of consumption changes in the long run. On this subject, see Chapter 5 below, pp. 114–15.

[16] For a description, see P. Sraffa, "The Laws of Return."

[17] *Ibid.*

independent of its supply. E. H. Chamberlin and Mrs. Robinson[18] later demonstrated that there existed equilibria other than the assumption of perfect competition and, in so doing, also showed that conditions of perfect competition are incompatible with the decision-making process within a capitalist enterprise. Other authors (e.g., Schumpeter) argued that capitalist growth is strictly dependent on the existence of monopolistic forms as centers of initiative large enough to determine the direction and pace of development. All these analyses are valid and have greatly enlarged economic knowledge. In fact, it is a great pity that so much hard work on market structures is now being ignored by the neomarginalist school. Facing the dilemma of the choice of assumptions as to market conditions, neomarginalists have unanimously decided to go back to that of perfect competition, on the basis that any other market structure would be equally arbitrary, and that the latter is an "optimum" in some sense or other.[19]

In any case, all that has been discovered about the incompatibility between the capitalist system and perfect competition cannot lead us to conclude that the *cause* of the differentiation of profit rates observed in the real world is the phenomenon of monopoly. Monopolistic market structures are obviously a necessary condition of a differentiated structure of profit rates, but they are not also a sufficient condition.[20] The differentiated structure of profit rates, then, could well be a logical first step in the development of monopolies, which would be the conclusion drawn from the argument that makes it dependent on long-term consumption trends.

One reason—and possibly the only one—that the existence of monopolies could also be considered a sufficient condition for the differentiation of profit rates is the presence of "natural" technical conditions favorable to the formation of monopolies. The capitalist system would then be "naturally" monopolistic, and monopolies would logically antedate the differentiation of profit rates. It has been argued, for instance, that one reason for the appearance of monopolistic structures is the existence of technological "disconti-

[18] E. H. Chamberlin, *Monopolistic Competition*; J. Robinson, *The Economics of Imperfect Competition* (London, 1933).

[19] True: perfect competition has been shown to be more efficient than other market forms in welfare economics, but this fact seems quite irrelevant; with the same logic a historian would be justified in assuming, while interpreting a historical incident, that men are moved by goodness rather than, say, self-interest, on the grounds that goodness is better than, say, self-interest or evil.

[20] This may be another reason why modern growth models so often assume conditions of perfect competition.

nuities" in production,[21] that is, the restriction of available plants to a few sizes. With regard to the quantity of a certain commodity produced, there would not be a complete range of productive capacities from size 0 to size X; therefore, the choice would be between plants with a productive capacity of, say, one thousand and plants with a productive capacity of, say, one hundred, within the same unit of time. Alternatively, with regard to the quantity of means of production employed, there would be only a few possible combinations of means of production (the production function is discontinuous). Obviously, if there are only a few technically feasible plant sizes, the "atomism" of supply (the condition that there must be an infinite number of suppliers) will not hold, and conditions of perfect competition will not be obtained. The entry of new enterprises onto the market then becomes difficult or even impossible, and the resulting monopolistic structure tends to maintain itself. This phenomenon is particularly relevant in our model, where the existence of various alternative techniques for the production of each commodity is excluded and only superior techniques are admitted.[22] If there exist technological discontinuities, and if a "natural monopoly" is formed, it is only logical to suppose that monopolists will tend to maintain it, especially because they do have a considerable influence over the determination of consumption.

There are two ways in which this tendency of monopolists can express itself: they can look for a production technique that will give them a natural monopoly, or they can try to increase consumption of commodities which sustain the natural monopoly they already possess. These two methods are in fact linked to each other, since with the growth of income the structure of consumption changes, and production techniques must also change.

In the first case, can entrepreneurs "order" their scientists or technicians to develop new production processes of a type that can constantly reinforce their natural monopoly? Entrepreneurs can always choose certain types of techniques over others, but their choice can only be exercised on the basis of the productivity of the techniques (output per unit of input), and there is no necessary re-

[21] Cf. P. Sylos-Labini, *Oligopolio e progresso tecnico* (Turin, 1957; English trans., *Oligopoly and Technical Progress*, Cambridge, Mass., 1962), chaps. ii and iii. See also F. Modigliani's review article, "New Developments on the Oligopoly Front," *Journal of Political Economy* (June, 1958).

[22] A definition is given below, Chapter 4, p. 71.

lationship between a technique's productivity and its ability to create natural monopolies. The assumption that entrepreneurs are capable of selecting a technique on the basis that it will require a certain quantity and composition of inputs, that it will give a certain total output, that it will be an optimum technique, and that it will prevent the entry of other enterprises into the industry is quite absurd. The production of commodities requires particular combinations of inputs which depend on mechanical, physical, and chemical laws. These combinations are "natural" and cannot be dictated by the entrepreneur so as to make the appearance of competition more difficult. As a result, natural monopolies are created and destroyed *at random* in all sectors of production without reference to the will of any individual entrepreneur. Natural monopolies are thus indifferent, in the long run and for a large number of technical changes, to the structure of the economic system. They will occur sometimes in one industry, sometimes in another, without a definite advantage ever being given to this or that industry. They cannot, therefore, be the cause of a permanently differentiated structure of profit rates.[23] We can, in fact, conclude that the natural monopolies described by the literature represent, in the long run, just what the neoclassical economists called a temporary disturbance in the conditions of perfect competition; these conditions, therefore, were it only for natural monopolies, would tend to be maintained in the long run.

In the second case, if monopolists had complete control over consumption, could they direct it so as always to maintain their original natural monopoly? This supposition is also absurd. With the growth of consumption—which follows Engel's law—the techniques necessary to provide the goods being demanded change constantly. Monopolists would thus have to develop newer and newer techniques of a type which would offer them a natural monopoly, and I have already commented on this. They could, alternatively, continually change the commodities they produce whenever a change of technique became necessary. But then consumption would not show any discernible trend, and Engel's law would not

---

[23] This argument can also be applied to economies of scale: even if they had been admitted in the present model, there does not seem to be a law which would make their occurrence more likely in one sector than in another; consequently, economies of scale would be distributed among sectors at random, in the long run, and should not influence the direction of the growth process.

be obeyed. Observation of reality, which clearly shows the existence of trends in the consumption of different commodities, also shows that there cannot be a relationship between technological discontinuities and natural monopolies on the one hand and the differentiation of profit rates on the other.[24]

GENERALIZATION OF THE DIFFERENTIATION OF PROFIT RATES

The above description of the process which creates a differential in profit rates throughout the economy was very simplified. In reality, there are many more industries than A and I. While the comparison between A and I helps to illustrate the basis of the formation of the differential, the process must be generalized to include all the industries present in the real world (or a representative sample of them). I am not capable of giving a mathematical illustration of a more general system, but it is not too difficult to extend the argument to a wider system.

Up to this point industries have been considered as independent from each other, in the sense that the commodities produced by I were not part of the inputs of A, and vice versa.[25] In other words, we have observed industries producing only for final consumption. But if we consider the economy as a whole, the case of independent industries becomes irrelevant. Let us consider a system wherein all commodities depend in various degrees on other commodities for their inputs. It will not be possible to show how a certain differential between profit rates of two industries is modified when all industrial interrelationships are taken into account, but it will be possible to demonstrate that a differential must also exist in the generalized model.

Let us return to the two-industry case and suppose that, among their inputs, industry I also uses commodity a and industry A also uses commodity i. In the long run, if consumption of the product of industry A grows at a slower rate than consumption of the commodities produced by I, A will show a lower profit rate than I. However, commodity a appears as an input of I. If the consumption of commodity i increases at a certain rate, the amount of means of

---

[24] If this is correct, then those theories (of Schumpeterian origin) which identify in natural monopolies the cause of the particular structure and growth process of capitalism would be invalid.

[25] Cf. however, p. 47, n. 8, above.

production used by I must change, and if *a* is part of the inputs of I, industry A will "participate" in the faster growth of the consumption of I in proportion to the quantity of *a* used in the increased production of *i*.[26] Conversely, if *i* is among the inputs of industry Λ, which confronts a consumption rising at a slower pace than that of *i*, industry I will "participate" in the slower growth of *a*'s consumption, in proportion to the quantity of *i* used in A. Therefore, once the technical interindustrial relationships are introduced, it will be the trend of total consumption (final consumption plus the use of inputs) confronted by each industry that determines the structure of profit rates, rather than the trend of final consumption alone. It is always possible to say that a differential among profit rates is maintained, even when the emphasis shifts from final consumption to total consumption. Given the structure and the development of technical interindustry relationships, the difference between the trends of consumption of *a* and of *i* will be maintained. This conclusion can be easily checked in the case where both commodities in the example are produced exclusively by means of wage goods which in turn are composed of only those two commodities. Total and final consumption are thus identical, by definition, and the total and final consumption of *i* will tend to increase faster than the total and final consumption of *a*, as income grows.

But apart from this limiting case, it is not possible to establish a simple law or rule for the composition of profit rates. Just to indicate the degree of complication which is found in passing from final to total consumption, the rate of profits in an industry relative to that of other industries depends upon what amount of the commodity produced by that industry (1) is used only as a wage good, the consumption of which increases at a higher, equal, or lower rate than the consumption of other wage goods; (2) is used only as an input other than wage goods, which enters into the production of both wage goods and other inputs, and whose total consumption depends upon the amount of final consumption of the commodity (or commodities) of which it is an input, as well as upon the extent to which it is used in the production of such a commodity (or commodities); and (3) is used both as a wage good and as an input other than a wage good, the total consumption of which depends both on its final consumption and on the final con-

---

[26] It is assumed that new techniques are adopted.

sumption of the commodities of which it is an input. The spectrum of possible combinations and interrelationships is quite large. In order to assess all the combinations, it would be necessary to build a system of simultaneous equations which, in the long run and with rising subsistence levels, would relate the rates of profits to consumption trends, as dictated by Engel's law, and to the technical structure of interindustry exchanges. Given the last two data, the rates of profits for all commodities could be determined.

If the assumption that wages always equal the psychological subsistence level is maintained, the net product of the system (the social surplus or the capitalists' income, in the simplified model) would be distributed among different industries not in direct proportion to the quantity of means of production employed, which would correspond to the state of uniform profit rates throughout the economy, but in proportion to the rate of growth of total consumption of each industry. The rates of profits in each industry would thus be determined by the income elasticity of the consumption of the commodity produced by each industry.

The rate of profit in each industry, however, will always be measured by reference to the means of production—capital—used. Now capital cannot be measured *after* prices are known because prices must reflect the structure of profit rates and, therefore, the value of capital. Capital cannot be measured *before* prices are known because, not being physically homogeneous, it must be expressed in terms of value. Prices and rates of profits must thus be determined simultaneously. If in the above description one could consider the technical structure of the economy and its changes as neutral, consumption and production as independent areas of activity, and the types of goods present on the market as given, there would, therefore, seem to be no problem: if outgo and income can be measured as suggested above, the prices of commodities would depend upon the same elements which determine the rates of profits.

As a result of the law of development of consumption, however, the price structure changes in the long run. Equilibrium, therefore, does not typically imply constancy of relative prices, but rather their change. This is the reason why any change in the techniques of production which influences the structure of relative prices in a way that does not correspond with the dynamics of consumption would interrupt the smooth development of relative prices in the long run. Similarly, if the independent actions of producers and consumers could effectively block the workings of the law of the development of consumption, they would represent an obstacle to the smooth functioning of the economic system. In this context, if Engel's law is the factor determining the structure of prices and profits in the long run, and if classical economists are right in assuming that changes in tastes are a consequence of the producer's action,[27] a fundamental contradiction takes shape.

Below (Chapters 4, 5, and 6) I shall consider the change in the technical structure, the relationship between the spheres of consumption and of production, and the role played by new goods. It will be seen that, for a number of reasons, it is not possible to build a system of simultaneous equations which permits a solution, *inter alia*, of the measurement problem.

RECONSIDERATION OF THE ECONOMIC LITERATURE

Does differentiation of profit rates help to solve the contradiction in the concept of value as embodied labor, as expressed by Ricardo and Marx? No, because the rates of profits in different industries are different, not in terms of the labor embodied in each commodity produced, but in terms of each commodity's consumption trend. Nor can we find any relationship between the trend in consumption of one commodity and the quantity of labor represented by that commodity. It is true that as income grows less essential needs will be satisfied, and that to satisfy these needs requires commodities which sometimes seem to be more "complicated," more "mechanized,"[28] but this observation can easily be extended to all types of commodities, including those the consumption of which rises less rapidly. One could perhaps suppose that technical progress has a tendency to be concentrated in industries which produce commodities the consumption of which grows most rapidly—and this point will be clarified below—but it would seem quite unsafe to rely on such an assumption in order to conclude that the greatest value (in the sense of embodied labor) is assigned to commodities the consumption of which rises at the fastest rate: technical interindustrial relationships also play a role in determining rates of profits, and the presence of a certain proportion of

[27] Schumpeter was in the same school of thought; see *Business Cycles* (New York, 1939), p. 74.

[28] A similar hypothesis is advanced by Spaventa ("Effetti di variazioni strutturali," p. 73).

commodity among the means of production of other commodities —which has an influence on the rate of profits of the industry producing the first commodity—cannot be easily placed in a systematic relationship with certain quantities of embodied labor.[29] This model, therefore, does not salvage the concept of value of Ricardo and Marx. If it is valid, then Mrs. Robinson's and Kaldor's models become largely invalid, while Sraffa's scheme loses its characteristic of simplicity.

In general, it is not possible to build models which show both a uniform profit rate (or a rate tending to uniformity) and a monopolistic market structure. It seems important to stress this contradiction because it has been often ignored. Yet unless one builds a quite unrealistic model entirely composed of absolute monopolies all having equal "power," it would be absurd to admit monopolistic structures which would then assure a structure of profit rates throughout the economy identical with that obtained by free competition. Even Marx appears to have committed this error. He does not try to modify the assumption of uniform profit rates when he analyzes monopolistic concentration in the third volume of *Das Kapital*. Similarly, many modern authors build their models on the assumption of free competition, and only after having described the characteristics of their constructions, including the uniformity of profit rates, do they complicate them by introducing monopolistic market forms.[30] But when the latter are introduced, the assumption of uniform profit rates, which derives from admitting free competition, is not re-examined. In general, there is a basic contrast between economic growth—which corresponds to the satisfaction of graduated needs—and the assumption of a proportional increase in the consumption of all the commodities of an economic system. If the trends in consumption are not duly taken account of, there is a serious risk of distorting economic interpretation.

CONCLUSION

I believe I have furnished a possible justification for the existence of a permanently differentiated structure of profit rates. In con-

---

[29] Unless Sraffa's model could be utilized.

[30] M. Kalecki (*Theory of Economic Dynamics* [London, 1954]) attempts an interpretation of capitalist income distribution based on the changes in the degree of monopoly of the system. The author, however, proceeds to aggregate the degree of monopoly of the different industries without examining its consequences on the rate of profits.

sidering the nature of this phenomenon, it may perhaps be useful to establish a parallel: as all individuals do not receive the same reward for the same effort and a disequilibrium system is not thereby created, so not all enterprises obtain the same profit for the same amount of investment. It should not, therefore, be too difficult to imagine an economy in which there exists a differentiated structure of profit rates rather than a uniform rate.

If a uniform profit rate does not exist, a uniform interest rate should not exist in a monetary universe. Although this differentiation is well known and has long been the subject of discussion—particularly since Keynes—it has always been related to the variability of interest rates in the short, medium, and long term, a variability variously interpreted as the result of uncertainty, risk, or time preference.[31] Although interest rates respond to forces and movements which are essentially different from those influencing the profit rates, particularly because the financial market does have characteristics and structures different from those of the production market, it appears intuitively clear that a relationship between profit rates and interest rates must exist. Risk premiums, for example, can be interpreted as rewards for those enterprises which best interpret, in their production plans, the natural diversification of the growth of the economy.

[31] S. A. Ozga ("Capital Resources, Equilibrium and Growth," *Economica* [November, 1962]) points out that economics has not yet provided a logical tool to deal with the case of different interest rates because of the universally accepted hypothesis of a uniform profit rate.

4

THE TECHNICAL
CONDITIONS
OF PRODUCTION

W̶e can now go back to the simple model sketched in Chapter 2, and observe the conditions and the nature of the capitalist development process. The starting point is the analysis of the technical conditions of production. It will be shown that technical change does not adversely influence the smooth growth of the capitalist system, even though it represents a necessary condition for such growth.

The time frame is, as usual, a long one. The model remains closed, and the assumption that the accumulation of capital is always sufficient to assure full employment will be maintained.

THE ORIGIN OF TECHNICAL PROGRESS

In the economic literature, technical progress is often considered to be a flow of innovations immediately applicable to production processes, almost as if it were simply a direct result of scientific-technological research. However, whatever the abundance of scientific research, the application of its results to the economy can only occur by means of a process of an economic nature. Technical progress is part of the economy only insofar as economic conditions are such that scientific-technical progress is made a part of the productive system. In other words, an innovation requires a conscious act by entrepreneurs in order to become an element of the economy, and no production method will be innovated, even though the scientific basis for it exists,[1] unless the economic system needs it. In this sense, scientific-technological progress is only a necessary condition, *not a sufficient one*, for the introduction of technical progress into the economy.

It is possible to state that the rhythm of technical progress—the rate at which innovations are introduced into the productive system—is a function, *inter alia*, of scientific research, and that this research, in turn, depends on the fact that enterprises set up re-

---

[1] As an example, one can cite the long interval between the discovery of electricity and the invention of the electric engine.

search laboratories. In other words, there exist laws of efficiency with regard to technical progress, and we shall consider one of them below. But this means only that enterprises are willing to innovate. The research of the economist must thus be directed toward the reasons for such willingness and the ways in which it becomes manifest, not toward the laboratories, which disappear from the economic scene. The concept of the entrepreneur will also include the technician; and what occurs in the economic process is the result of what entrepreneurs demand—implicitly or explicitly —of their technicians, not what the technicians offer to entrepreneurs.

I define technical progress (which includes here also the phenomenon of economies of scale) to include not only the invention of a new machine or a new productive process or the discovery of mechanical, physical, and chemical principles as applied to production, but also the change in the productive organization (an enterprise, an industry, or the economy as a whole) brought about by the change in the specifications of existing productive factors. For example, I will consider as technical progress (if, of course, a productive advantage is in fact obtained) both the invention of the locomotive and of the factory system of production—the latter even if it is based on existing production techniques.

The general reason why entrepreneurs desire technical progress, though simple, is at the foundation of the growth process. For each entrepreneur, technical progress is nothing more than a reduction of production costs (per unit of output); it represents, therefore, an attempt to increase the rate of profits on invested capital. As such, the motive for the introduction of technical progress is similar to the profit motive.

This is only one reason for technical progress, however. In the long run there exists an autonomous device for the introduction of new techniques. Since the subsistence level of consumption will rise, entrepreneurs face a long-run tendency towards lower profits unless technical progress is made. In turn, the long-run tendency to introduce innovations permits wages to rise. There is thus a basis for concluding that there exists a long-term mechanism which reconciles the profit motive and the rise of the subsistence level (see also below).

THE ROLE OF TECHNICAL PROGRESS

One of the fundamental principles of marginalist thought, as well as of most of the contemporary literature,[2] is that at each moment of time there exist many alternative production techniques (a production function both at the level of the enterprise and of the economy as a whole). A choice among these techniques would be made by entrepreneurs on the basis of the relative rates of profits and wages prevailing at the moment. The various techniques present at a given time would be ranked according to their productivity (in terms of output per man), *the technique with higher productivity either requiring a greater investment per man or, with equal investment, giving a lower total output* relative to other techniques. Insofar as these techniques require a higher investment per man than other techniques, they are defined as having a *higher degree of mechanization*.[3] No technique, however, would be *superior* to others (otherwise it would be chosen automatically in preference to any other), in the sense that no technique could show, with equal investment, a greater output per man *and* the same or higher total output; nor, with equal amounts of labor employed, could any technique show a higher output per unit of investment *and* an equal or higher total output in comparison with other techniques.[4]

According to the marginalists, therefore, economic growth would occur by means of a process which combines changes in the degree of mechanization[5] in each branch of production, deriving from

---

[2] See, for example, J. Robinson, *Accumulation of Capital*, p. 70: "Changes in technique are considered in two separate categories, those which arise from inventions and discoveries and those which are due to changes in wages relative to profits in a given state of technical knowledge. The separation is somewhat artificial, for in reality the two types of change are inextricably mingled, but for analytical purposes the distinction is helpful." Kaldor, as we have seen, does not accept this distinction. It is also lacking in the well-known Harrod-Domar model; see R. F. Harrod, *Towards a Dynamic Economics* (London, 1948), pp. 77 and ff., and E. D. Domar, *Essays in the Theory of Economic Growth* (New York, 1957), Vol. III. See also K. J. Arrow, "The Economic Implications of Learning by Doing," *Review of Economic Studies* (June, 1962).

[3] Also called "capital deepening." For a graphic illustration of these definitions, see Appendix B, p. 158.

[4] For a brief but clear exposition of the neoclassical and neomarginalist models, see K. Ara, "Capital Theory and Economic Growth," *Economic Journal* (September, 1958).

[5] A symmetrical process of "capital shallowing" or demechanization is conceivable. However, it should not have great importance in this model, since the history of capitalism has always been interpreted in terms of a process of mechanization (linked to a continuous rise in wages). On the other hand, the lesser importance of capital shallowing is also a necessity:

changes in wages relative to profits, with the tendency towards superior techniques—technical progress proper—caused by factors outside the economic system.[6] In the neoclassical model, this process can be expressed as the combination of movements along the production function with shifts in the function itself. It is therefore admitted that each innovation not only creates one new technique but also affects the entire spectrum of available alternative techniques, in such a way as to create a complete new spectrum of techniques—superior in relation to the old spectrum—within which entrepreneurs would again make a selection among techniques with varying degrees of mechanization.

Before we extend this critique to fundamentals, let us briefly stop here and assess the realism of assuming that an innovation affects the whole spectrum of existing techniques and creates a new one. In its purest expression, the marginalist production function is a continuous curve, representing an infinity of alternative techniques. Many economists have attempted to improve the degree of realism of such a curve[7] and have built models based on only a few techniques, where choice is possible but restricted. These models are interesting because they leave room for positions of disequilibrium. They do not, however, remedy the unreality of the neoclassical formulation because even where the production function is discontinuous, technical progress would create a whole new spectrum, and why technical progress should create more than one technique is not clear. However, the marginalist theory cannot admit that technical progress gives rise to only one technique at a time: as will be shown below, its basic principle and one of the pillars of its philosophy would be destroyed if this were admitted.

It is interesting to observe at this point that, since we have made Engel's law on the development of consumption the basis of the dynamics of prices, if reality in fact did show many alternative techniques among which entrepreneurs could choose, the system of relative prices—and therefore of profit rates—would logically take precedence over the choice of techniques, and entrepreneurial choices would already be determined. This situation could yield an

---

for this process to be continuous it is necessary that in the past there has been mechanization.

[6] I maintain the assumption that technical progress is spread evenly throughout the economy in the long run.

[7] Robinson, *Accumulation of Capital, passim*; R. S. Eckaus, "Factor Proportions in Underdeveloped Areas," *American Economic Review* (September, 1955).

equilibrium system. However, we shall have occasion to see that reality is not so simple.

The foundation of the neoclassical choice rests on the Ricardian law of diminishing returns to continued use of one productive factor when all others are fixed. This law has a suggestive plausibility and has never been radically doubted. A few economists have indicated that the law manifests itself only in certain circumstances. It does not apply, for example, in the cases of rigid factor mix—of non-substitutability of factors—but these circumstances have been considered the exception rather than the rule.

In these pages the Ricardian law will be systematically put into question. Thus I shall abandon the notion of combination of inputs and adopt the notion of *productive technique*. A technique is a particular combination of factors of production used in the production of one commodity or of a group of commodities, the quantity and quality of which factors have previously been studied (scientifically as well as technically) and have then been embodied in a *plant*. Each plant produces a certain quantity—and quality—of a commodity. In my model it is not possible to increase the quantity produced by a plant in a unit of time by increasing one or more—but not all—of the elements which make up the plant. If some of the economic variables (wages, profits, prices) were to change and the plant should become unprofitable (or less profitable), it would be necessary to change the plant. This requires an innovating effort.

When technical progress is introduced into the picture, it manifests itself in a new technique and in a new plant or series of plants, and these plants do not follow the law of diminishing returns. For a new plant to be subject to the law of diminishing returns, it is necessary that the innovation produce a series of new techniques which are not superior in relation to each other, and which are alternative in the sense that a larger or smaller utilization of certain factors of production may affect their profitability. But unless the availability of non-superior techniques is due to chance, it may be difficult, as will be shown below, to admit it as a logical possibility. Since the creation of such flexibility in a plant itself requires an innovative effort, it is much more probable—given the more favorable result—that this effort will be directed toward obtaining superior techniques. This is why I find it difficult to believe that an innovation creates a complete new spectrum of techniques, rather than only one technique.

In short, it is true that the marginalist argument based on the unlimited substitutability of factors of production can also be applied to the case in which there are few possible factor combinations without loss of its general validity.[8] But if there existed only one possible technique at any given moment of time—a technique superior to any other, whatever the rate of profits and wages—the marginalist argument could not be applied.

That there is more than one technique of production available in each moment of time and that they are such that no one is superior to any other has been a common assertion in economics, as we have seen, since the advent of marginalism. However, this assertion has never been subject to a direct statistical proof. It could not have been, notwithstanding its plausibility, since it is impossible to prove the existence of an instantaneous production function *a priori*.[9] The statistical exercises based on the Cobb-Douglas function, as well as on other fitting equations, cannot hope to prove that a production function exists. Insofar as they are within the limit of statistical confidence, they can only prove that at the moment of the

[8] However, F. Troughton ("Production Costs in Introductory Economics," *Journal of Industrial Economics* [April, 1963], pp. 105–8) gives some interesting examples of the impossibility of choosing the optimum combination of inputs and of the lack of "intermediate" techniques.

[9] On pp. 4–8 the vicious circle which undermines the neoclassical production function was illustrated, at the level of the economy as a whole. It was also said that for each entrepreneur the function could still be valid, but it was observed that without the possibility of aggregating the functions relating to each enterprise, the function for the individual enterprise does not have much meaning. Particularly in a world composed of monopolistic forms, even if the production function of one monopolist were known, it could not be determined empirically. The function is expressed at current prices, and since these prices reflect, *inter alia*, the technique used by the monopolist under consideration, if he changes the technique all the relationships forming the price system will change, and the production functions before and after this change will not be comparable. The rate of profits yielded by the technique used by the entrepreneur before the change will be different from the profit rate yielded by the new technique because the latter will have changed all the conditions of profitability. The more monopolistic is the enterprise, the more important this is. Although each monopolist is capable of calculating, more or less approximately, the effects of his actions on the economy as a whole and therefore is able to see the relationship between inputs and output, the external observer will not be able to reconstruct the choices made by the individual entrepreneur by means of a production function derived empirically (and thus *a posteriori*). The external observer is usually excluded from observation of these phenomena: even if the complex of aims of the class and/or Engel's law substitute for the production function as laws of value, it will not be possible to give them a quantitative expression *a priori* (see Chapters 5 and 6).

statistical check the data arranged themselves in a fashion not too dissimilar from that of a production function, and this result can occur for a number of reasons which may have little to do with the marginalist theory of production.

I shall try to demonstrate, on purely logical grounds, that in fact there is only one technique in each moment of time. A statistical proof of this alternative formulation is lacking. It remains, however, a legitimate alternative, precisely because no other theory has been proved. Furthermore, this alternative may have a stronger logical appeal, and is certainly a simpler formulation, than that of the marginalists. I cannot establish its degree of plausibility, but I suspect that plausibility is determined more by long-established tradition and general usage than by nearness to truth. For the sake of simplicity, only one sector of production will be examined. The argument can be extended to all the sectors of a complex economy.

I strongly suspect that marginalists and neomarginalists confuse the requirements of analysis and reality. They study the growth process at a given moment and, observing in such a moment a plurality of techniques, they conclude that entrepreneurs must make a choice among them. It is easy, once this conclusion is made, to reconstruct, *ex post facto*, imaginary criteria that entrepreneurs would adopt in choosing a technique (arguing at the same time that whether they in fact do so or not is irrelevant), and to postulate enterprises which change their production processes continually according to the relative change in the rate of profits and the wage rate. However, when the economy is analyzed at a given moment of time, it is impossible to say with assurance whether the plurality of techniques bring about entrepreneurial decisions, or whether entrepreneurial decisions bring about, or have brought about, the plurality of techniques. Each step in the development process derives from historical decisions made earlier. Only by retracing the historical decision-making process could one determine which is the causative element, the entrepreneurial decision or the variety of techniques.

Let us start from an economy in which there is only one technique of production.[10] Entrepreneurs are always looking for a new technique which will increase productivity and raise their profits.

[10] The following argument was developed in part by the author in "Tecniche di produzione, progresso tecnico e sviluppo economico," *Rivista internazionale di scienze economiche e commerciali* (June, 1962).

But entrepreneurs who are trying to modify the technical conditions of production face the *same difficulty, from a technological point of view, whether they attempt to obtain a superior technique or a technique with a higher (or lower) degree of mechanization.* Both the superior technique and the more (or less) mechanized one must be created *ex novo*; both are completely new production processes from the technological standpoint, requiring types and quantities of machines and labor different than the technique previously employed. When technical progress is observed over time, *starting from only one technique at the initial moment*, there cannot be substitutability among factors of production, and each new combination of factors requires an original inventive effort. Under these conditions, it would seem obvious that entrepreneurs will always demand superior techniques of their scientists.

It can be objected that this superiority criterion is not valid if non-superior techniques were available from the initial moment of the development process. The objection can be dismissed. Non-superior techniques must also be invented. Their presence at the initial moment of the development process would imply that some time before there had been a systematic search for and a choice of new techniques. But if at that "pre-initial" moment there was only one technique available, then only superior techniques would be invented and adopted afterwards, assuming equal difficulty in creating superior and non-superior techniques. If at that "pre-initial" moment, on the other hand, there were many non-superior techniques, then at a still earlier moment there must have been a systematic search for new techniques. As a result, it is not legitimate to argue that at the initial moment of the development process there were many non-superior techniques without pushing that initial moment further back into the past; and *to avoid an infinite (and logically absurd) backward movement*, it is necessary to postulate only one technique at the initial moment of the process. At that moment, therefore, there did not exist in each production line a body of alternative techniques which could be chosen, depending upon their degree of mechanization, but only one technique, the traditional and primitive one. At that point in time (logically, rather than chronologically, interpreted), if entrepreneurs had had to decide between creating a superior technique or creating a technique with a higher or lower degree of mechanization, since the technological difficulty is the same in both cases, they would have searched for, and adopted, only superior techniques.

This argument is further strengthened when one considers that, even admitting the existence of many non-superior techniques at one moment of time, the introduction of technical progress—no matter how it is brought about—will result, at least occasionally, in *one* superior technique rather than in a *spectrum* of alternative techniques which neither the technician nor the entrepreneur set out to obtain; and from the moment in which that superior technique is introduced in a production line, it is only reasonable to suppose that superior techniques will be adopted afterwards.

Economic growth is a chronological affair. If the initial situation is as described above, in each subsequent moment the situation will continue to be as in the initial one; enterprises will successively adopt only techniques which are superior to former ones and will always be about to scrap the present technique in favor of a superior one. Logical continuity imposes the rule that what is valid for the first choice is also valid for any future choice. The process has been repeated many times in the past and is being repeated at present; looking back, one can easily observe that a large number of techniques has been used even though, in each moment, there is only one prevalent technique.

In the real world, the passage from one technique to the other does not happen simultaneously in all lines of production and in all enterprises. Inferior techniques can be present by the side of superior techniques in the same industry, since the speed with which technical progress is evaluated and adopted by different entrepreneurs is bound to vary. For these and other reasons mentioned above, the observer of the technical scene at one moment in time will notice that more than one technique seems to be available.

It could be said, when looking at the "research" laboratory, that scientists and technicians may well produce a complex of possible new techniques, rather than only one, among which the entrepreneur can choose. If the entrepreneur is bent only on increasing his profit without caring about the way in which such an increase is obtained, that complex could well include both superior and non-superior techniques.[11] If superior and non-superior techniques are present at the same time, entrepreneurs will normally choose superior ones. However, if they make a mistake and choose a non-superior one, they will again be facing a neoclassical choice. How-

---

[11] Appendix B explains why the presence of superior techniques which are at the same time in a non-superior relationship cannot be admitted.

ever, there is no reason to suppose that such mistakes are more than random happenings without permanent consequences. Such a mistake, in any case, cannot really parallel the neoclassical choice because it is made when a superior technique is available and can always be corrected.

One cannot exclude the possibility that, from time to time, the mix of techniques furnished by the research laboratory may include only more or less mechanized techniques, and no superior techniques; but even in such an instance the neoclassical choice is not duplicated. As soon as the more (or less) mechanized technique is to be changed, the research laboratory will furnish, as normally it would, superior techniques, alone or along with non-superior ones. One can therefore say that the presence from time to time of a more (or less) mechanized technique is an exception confirming the rule that technical conditions of production change only through the adoption of superior techniques.

Moreover, it is necessary to free ourselves from the image of the entrepreneur as a subject at the mercy of the scientist and incapable of expressing his economic preference in technological terms. We have already observed that the concept of entrepreneur includes the research laboratory. We also have established that the tendency to maximize is the springboard of entrepreneurial decisions. Although once a new technique has been chosen an entrepreneur knows its effect on the economy only approximately, he should be clearly aware, both in research and in application, of the difference between superior and non-superior techniques at the level of his enterprise; the latter can be optimal only at a given level and structure of factor prices, while the former are optimal at any set of factor prices. If the assumption is made that the entrepreneur is denied this insight, *he should also be denied the ability to choose among techniques having different degrees of mechanization.*

The definition of technical progress given in the preceding paragraphs excludes all those improvements which occur independent of entrepreneurial will and which, in our model, cannot be properly considered to be technical progress even though they may contribute to an increase in productivity. I am referring in particular to the great number of improvements introduced by workers, technicians, administrators, etc., in the machines, tools, and organizations at which they work, improvements which are quite independent of the economic situation of the enterprise or of the industry.

These improvements cannot be classified according to their effects on the economy, both because of their varied character and because they are not the result of a conscious choice. Then too, these improvements should represent a chance event with neutral effects on the economy, and should not affect my argument.

My interpretation of the change in technical conditions of production, although perhaps possessing some logical force, cannot be applied *sic et simpliciter* to concrete economic situations, without the likelihood of rendering it a tautology. There are some economic factors in which the technical element is in practice only vaguely definable (a typical example is that of administrative capacities). In the treatment above, it is implicitly assumed that those elements are technical in nature. There are also other factors (geographical, climatic, historical, etc.) which can neither be considered as technical elements nor as constants. The latter can probably be treated as random variables in the long run, and should not influence in any direction the change in technical conditions.[12] In conclusion, technical progress is regarded here as the only factor influencing in a permanent fashion the technical conditions of production.[13] The neoclassical production function has been stripped of all its meaning.

[12] The argument for the existence of only one superior technique in each production line can also be expressed by saying that the application of further amounts of inputs (such as labor) at best leaves output unchanged. It would thus be reasonable to think that, at least in agriculture (where it is easier to observe that the application of further quantities of labor to a certain amount of land may increase total output), our concept of equal difficulty in using superior and in using non-superior techniques loses its validity. I have not studied this question in depth. It would seem to me, however, that starting from the moment in which the agricultural sector underwent technical changes—became subject, that is, to technical progress, such as the utilization of machinery, fertilizers, etc.—my concept would be fully applicable. G. S. Tolley and S. Smidt ("Agriculture and the U.S. Economy," *Econometrica* [October, 1964]) state that the pattern of the elasticity of substitution among inputs bought by the farm changes in completely unforeseeable ways at the change of the input mix.

[13] Those who will not be able to renounce the concept of the production function will have to admit that in a period as long as that set forth in these pages the instantaneous variability of techniques disappears to make a place for technical progress. M. Abramowitz (*Resources and Output Trends in the United States since 1870* [National Bureau of Economic Research Occasional Paper 52; New York, 1956]) states that the cause of the large increase in per capita net output has not been so much the increase in capital outputs per capita, but rather the complex of those "not yet well understood" forces which have given rise to the increase in productivity.

THE PACE OF TECHNICAL PROGRESS

As a result of the profit motive, technical progress is continually introduced in the economy. Let us briefly examine a few questions relating to the rhythm with which technical progress replaces obsolete techniques with new ones.

In the presence of steady technical progress, each time it is necessary to renew a plant—when its useful physical life is exhausted—the new plant will embody all those technical improvements which have been invented and made technically feasible during the lifetime of the old plant. Technical progress, however, does not affect only fixed installations, but working capital as well. It can also occur in the form of improvements immediately applicable to obsolete plants.

In any case, it is not necessary that old plants should have completely exhausted their production potential before they are replaced by new and superior plants. For this to happen it is necessary that the profits of the new plant cover, as an additional cost, the discounted profits which could have been obtained from the old plant, and that the resulting profit rate, after adjusting for such cost element, be higher than the rate obtained from the old plant.

From these brief observations one can conclude that the technical life span of plants does have a role—albeit modest—in determining the rhythm of technical progress. The converse problem, namely, whether technical progress affects the average life of plants, should be given an even larger role. A longer or shorter average life of plants brought about by technical progress can be interpreted *mutatis mutandis* as representing lower or higher capital intensities, namely, capital-saving or capital-using biases. These problems are dealt with below.

THE CHARACTER OF TECHNICAL PROGRESS

It is now necessary to analyze critically the assumption of uniform distribution of technical progress among the different sectors of the economy. There are two ways of looking at this question, also called the determination of the "character" of technical progress. On the one hand, it is possible to say that the character of technical progress is such as to change the relationships among the sectors of the economy from what they were before the introduction of new techniques. On the other hand, it is conceivable that entrepreneurs may want technical progress of a particular character, more "profitable" or more "convenient" for them. These two components of the question can be studied together: it will be sufficient to examine the technical progress function for the economy as a whole and ascertain whether and how it could be influenced by entrepreneurial decisions. In order to analyze this function, it is necessary to define the character that technical progress can acquire. I shall follow Mrs. Robinson's terminology.[14]

Neutral is that technical progress by which output per man em-

[14] Robinson, *Accumulation of Capital*, pp. 97–99, 131–33, and 164–71. There is a very large body of literature on the character of technical progress, and it directly derives from the general discussion on growth problems. Beginning with the neoclassical approach of J. R. Hicks in *The Theory of Wages* (London, 1932) and with the new definitions of Harrod in *Towards a Dynamic Economics*, the discussion has occupied a great number of economists. The problem has become even more difficult because each author has chosen his own definitions. But the difficulties are not only in nomenclature. C. Kennedy ("The Character of Improvements and of Technical Progress," *Economic Journal* [December, 1962]) has shown under what conditions Harrod's and Hicks's definitions become identical. The interest in the problem of the character of innovations was also stimulated by statistical analyses (see, *inter alia*, S. Kuznets, "Long Term Changes in the National Income of the United States since 1870," in Kuznets and R. Goldsmith, *Income and Wealth in the United States: Trends and Structure* [Cambridge, 1952]), which, in studying the economies of advanced countries, pointed out that the aggregate incremental capital-output ratio and the shares of wages and profits in national income remain approximately constant in the long run. If the share of profits and the incremental capital-output ratio are constant, the "average" rate of return on investment will also remain constant. The constancy of these ratios would indicate that while there is a continuous rise in the capital-labor ratio, labor productivity has also risen (*pari passu*) and is increasing at the same rate in both sector K and sector C, indicating neutral technical progress. These statistical results have been doubted: see, for example, E. H. Phelps-Brown and P. E. Hart, "The Share of Wages in National Income," *Economic Journal* (June, 1952); R. M. Solow, "A Skeptical Note on the Constancy of Relative Shares," *American Economic Review* (September, 1958); I. B. Kravis, "Relative Income Shares in Fact and in Theory," *ibid.* (December, 1959); L. Klein and R. F. Kosubud, "Some Econometrics of Growth: Great Ratios of Economics," *Quarterly Journal of Economics* (May, 1961). In any case, it is unsafe to trust statistical analyses, primarily because of the impossibility of measuring capital and output in the long run. To conclude, for example, that the capital-output ratio has shown a certain trend, after studying statistical series which have been deflated by taking into account changes in the level (and structure) of prices, means to rediscover, under a different name, the hypotheses previously made with regard to prices. This difficulty has been pointed out also by V. V. Bhatt, "Aggregate Capital-Output Ratio: Some Conceptual Issues," *Indian Economic Journal* (April, 1963). The criticism also applies, of course, to those statistical studies which intend to demonstrate the variability (in one or the other direction) of the capital-output ratio. On this topic, see A. Grant, "Issues in Distribution Theory: The Measurement of Labor's Relative Share 1899–1929," *Review of Economics and Statistics* (August, 1963).

ployed (productivity) increases in the same proportion in the sector producing investment goods (K) and in the sector producing consumer goods (C). In other words, technical progress is neutral when it reduces the quantity of labor necessary to produce and maintain capital goods in the same proportion as it reduces the quantity of labor necessary to man the capital goods. Technical progress will show a *capital-using* (labor-saving) bias when productivity in sector K rises more slowly than productivity in sector C; it will show a *capital-saving* (labor-using) bias when productivity in K rises more rapidly than productivity in C. Thus, technical progress has a capital-using bias when the quantity of labor necessary to produce and maintain capital goods is reduced less than the quantity of labor necessary to man the capital goods; it has a capital-saving bias when the quantity of labor necessary to produce and maintain capital goods is reduced more than the quantity of labor necessary to man those capital goods.

These definitions can also be expressed in another way.[15] Let us suppose that an innovation introduced in an enterprise producing consumer goods requires the same investment as the technique it replaces, but yields a larger output[16] (assuming that the physical life expectancy of the plant does not change). As a result, output per man in sector C, in terms of consumer goods, and output per man in sector K, in terms of units of productive capacity of consumer goods, grow at the same rate, and technical progress is neutral. If, on the other hand, the innovation increases output but reduces the investment necessary to set up the new technique, output per man in K, again measured in units of productive capacity of consumer goods, increases at a greater rate than output per man in C. Technical progress will then have a capital-saving bias.[17]

In a market where competitive conditions prevail, even though it is the entrepreneur who seeks and adopts technical progress, no single entrepreneur possesses such wide decision-making power or such an overwhelming will as to be able to influence the character of technical progress in one sense or the other. In this case, technical progress must be neutral. If there is no reason why sector K or sec-

---

[15] Cf. Robinson, *Essays in the Theory of Economic Growth* (London, 1962), pp. 90–91.

[16] It is assumed that output can be measured.

[17] Mrs. Robinson (*Accumulation of Capital*, p. 419) gives a graphic exposition of the neutrality criterion, which may be useful here (Appendix B further clarifies the question).

tor C should show alternative increases in productivity, in the long run and for a great number of innovations technical progress will distribute itself at random among its three characteristics. Therefore, the character of technical progress can be considered *a random variable that takes three values* (neutral, capital-saving, or capital-using) *with constant probability,* the average value of which necessarily corresponds to its neutral character.[18]

A preference or a choice among the characteristics of technical progress on the part of entrepreneurs could perhaps be admitted to the extent that a monopolistic market structure replaces a competitive one. In this case, the entrepreneur would be able to calculate —although only approximately—the effects of his own action on the economy as a whole and on his own monopolistic enterprise. Although his view is only partial, some degree of judgment ought to be assumed to be present. However, since the character of technical progress changes insofar as it influences, to varying degrees, the productivities of sectors K and C, a monopolist can choose technical progress only if he controls the whole production of sec-

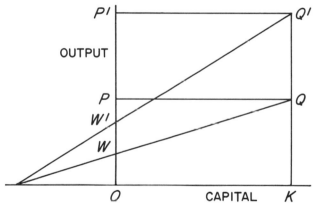

In the figure, the ordinate indicates output per man and the abscissa capital per man (measured in terms of wage units). If the labor force is given, the axes represent total output and total capital. Taking OW as the (real) wage and Q as the technique in use, the value of capital in terms of commodities will be given by $OW \times OK$ and the "average" rate of profits by $WP : OW \times OK$. Technical progress will be neutral in the case of new technique Q', for which the real wage (OW') has risen in the same proportion of output (OP'), the rate of profit remains constant ($WP : OW \times OK = W'P' : OW' \times OK$), and the capital-output ratio is also constant ($OW \times OK : OP = OW' \times OK : OP'$).

[18] The possible effects of biased innovations are briefly examined in Appendix B, p. 161.

tors K and C.[19] He should, in other words, control the whole economic system, which contradicts the definition of a capitalist economy.

We could, alternatively, imagine that the entrepreneurial class—rather than individual entrepreneurs—is capable of choosing the character of technical progress. However, while the class exercises its control in the long run and at discrete intervals, the introduction of technical progress is a continual phenomenon, the choice of which would imply the existence of formal decision-making organs which are not present in reality. In addition, since in the case of technical progress the aims of individual entrepreneurs do not necessarily complement each other—because if they are in conflict technical progress will take on a neutral character without disturbing the orderly growth of the system—entrepreneurs will not act in the same way, and the class need not assume the role of regulator of the economy. Finally, a choice of the character of technical progress would depend not only on entrepreneurs' class consciousness, but also on their ability to recognize sectors K and C. But the breakdown of the economy into sectors (K, C, or any other division) is purely analytical and is not part of economic reality. It cannot, therefore, be assumed that entrepreneurs seek a special type of technical progress, depending on whether it influences sectors of production which they do not recognize in reality.[20] Thus it seems reasonable to suppose that technical progress will be neutral in character even in a monopolistic market structure.

It is clearly possible to conceive that there exists a general entrepreneurial tendency to substitute machines for men. Marx thought that, as a result of this tendency, the reserve army of unemployed would be re-created each time real wages exceeded the subsistence level. In fact, technical progress may well continue to be neutral even in the presence of such a tendency, since the substitution of machines for men would occur in the same fashion through the whole economy.

This exposition of the conditions for neutrality of technical progress is, obviously, very rough, and a thorough examination of the phenomenon would require an analysis of past events as they have

---

[19] In Appendix B it is shown that even complete control of the economy does not necessarily mean that the character of technical progress can be determined.

[20] The existence of vertically integrated monopolies is proof of the impossibility of recognizing sectors K and C in the real world.

happened. This is not possible here, both because I did not set out to give a statistical proof of my hypotheses and because a statistical proof would most likely shatter itself against the measurement problem.

In conclusion, technical conditions of production change with the continual adoption of superior techniques. The economy as a whole will find itself at a superior level if the accumulation of capital is always sufficient to maintain full employment. The new techniques will be neutral, in the long run, and will not alter the relationships of the sectors of the economy, the "average" rate of profits, or the shares of profits and wages (if the latter exceed the subsistence level) in real output.

THEORIES OF INDUCED INNOVATION

In this interpretive model, entrepreneurs have not been given power sufficient to determine the character of technical progress. But there exist a number of theories that attempt to interpret the new techniques as the result of conscious entrepreneurial choices or, at least, of natural entrepreneurial tendencies. Of course, if the character of techniques is not subject to enterprise planning, no theory is needed. This seems to be Mrs. Robinson's conclusion, although she does not try to discover what would be, in the circumstances, the most likely result.

J. R. Hicks[21] was the first to propose that a change in the relative price of factors can influence the character of new techniques. Lately, C. Kennedy has proposed that the choice of new techniques is influenced by the shares of labor and capital represented in the unit cost of a commodity; the higher the share of labor, the more the entrepreneur will search for labor-saving (capital-using) innovations.[22] Following this proposition and given a sufficiently large number of innovations, whatever the relative shares of the two factors to begin with, the neutral position becomes the equilibrium position (and a stable one). Unfortunately, Kennedy's proposition has been shown to be valid only in a special set of circumstances.[23] In addition, as a behavioral interpretation, Kennedy's idea seems quite weak (and Hicks's is no stronger). If instead of just two

[21] *The Theory of Wages.*

[22] Kennedy, "Induced Bias in Innovation and the Theory of Distribution," *Economic Journal* (September, 1964).

[23] See S. Ahmed, "On the Theory of Induced Invention," *Economic Journal* (June, 1966).

factors, the entrepreneur were to choose among *n* factors—which is a closer approximation of reality—relative factor shares or relative factor prices would not be so clearly identifiable. Capital is individualized in a number of particular machines; labor is individualized in a number of particular skills.[24] All the shares and prices of these machines and skills would play a part in the choice of new techniques; but would an entrepreneur be able to demand from his scientist-technicians an innovation or a series of innovations which would reduce the shares of the "high-share" inputs in proportion to the relative level of each share? Or, to reverse the proposition, would it make sense that entrepreneurs would order their scientist-technicians to develop new techniques which would not reduce the shares of "low-share" factors? The number of choices open to entrepreneurs in selecting the character of innovations becomes so great that the whole theory acquires an aura of unreality.

The theories which would make the character of technical progress a function of factor prices or of factor shares are, of course, relevant to our interpretative model. They imply that the relative scarcity of one factor determines the direction of technical progress. This is a plausible conclusion, but it derives directly from an economic model of the neoclassical type. As was already shown, this conclusion will not hold up under examination. Whether or not there are behavioral laws controlling the choice of the character of new techniques at the level of each enterprise, there is still no reason to suppose that the consumption or investment sectors would win in the scramble. In any event, since technical progress already gives entrepreneurs techniques which are superior to any other available technique at *any* set of relative factor prices, it does not seem reasonable to suppose that they are so forward looking as to be able to choose the character of techniques they do not yet have.

TECHNICAL PROGRESS AND
THE DIFFERENTIATION OF PROFIT RATES

Let us now turn to the question of whether the change in the technical conditions of production can affect in a permanent way the differentiation of profit rates, and/or whether the differentia-

---

[24] The well-known fact that labor is less individualized than capital in factory production would, according to Kennedy's theory, impart a natural labor-saving bias to all innovations, a result certainly not desired by the author.

tion of profit rates can affect the change in technical conditions. As a result of the discussion above, we see that techniques will change only as a result of the introduction of technical progress. We retain the assumption that the rate of capital accumulation is always adequate to maintain full employment. Since the consumption of the commodities produced by industries A and I increases, even though at different rates for the two commodities, and since the economy is at full employment, each output increase can only come about by means of the introduction of superior techniques.[25]

If technical progress was adopted only in one industry, or at a greater rate in one industry than in another, the relationship among production costs of the industries and the structure of prices would change. Technical progress would not be neutral.[26] Similarly, technical progress would not be neutral if the research for new techniques were stimulated to a higher degree in industry I, which faces a consumption which grows at a faster rate and which is, therefore, more monopolistic.

The differentiation mechanism among profit rates is a continuous process in which the adoption of new techniques originates from the increase in consumption, under full employment conditions, and from the tendency of entrepreneurs to obtain the maximum profit rate. If the latter is an accepted postulate, then the following lemma must also be accepted. The maximum profit tendency acts with the same intensity also within each class, in a system of *classes* of profit. Monopolistic forms have the ability only to separate classes, not to abolish or modify their tendency to accumulate.[27] In this way, the push to obtain technical progress—which is only another aspect of the push to accumulate—will be greatest and even in all industries.

However, even if the search for technical progress is carried out with the same intensity in all industries and in all classes of profit, the result in terms of new superior techniques need not be equal in all industries. In examining this problem, industries must be classified not on the basis of *absolute* size (invested capital, sales,

[25] For the necessity of this assumption, see p. 94.

[26] In this case, "neutral" means that technical progress is indifferent with respect to the system of relative prices.

[27] See S. P. Dobrovolsky (*Corporate Income Retention 1915–1943* [New York, 1951]) and S. G. Prais ("Some Problems of Econometric Analysis of Company Accounts" [18th European Congress of the Econometric Society, 1956]) conclude that the propensity to save is approximately the same irrespective of the size of enterprises.

etc.), which is not necessarily relevant in a dynamic context, but on the basis of the rate of change in the absolute size. Where industries grow faster, the rate of profits will be larger, even though the absolute size of profits will not necessarily be larger. It should be possible, on this basis, to establish an "efficiency law" of technical progress: the faster the rate of increase of investment in research for new techniques, the greater the rate of increase in technical progress will be. Since the rate of increase in investment is greater for industries which face a consumption rising at a faster rate, it can be said that technical progress will appear to a greater degree in industries where the rate of profits is higher.[28] Although this is a case of "non-neutrality" in technical progress,[29] it is not disruptive of the dynamic equilibrium of the price system. On the contrary, it can be considered a principal means by which equilibrium is continually reconstituted, within the variations of consumption brought about by Engel's law. Since industry I is also more monopolistic, the "greater" technical progress it obtains will be reflected not so much in lower prices for its products as in a greater self-financing capacity. Conversely, industries which confront a stagnant level of consumption, or one that rises more slowly than that of other industries, will obtain "less" technical progress. The adjustment of productive sectors and relative prices to the changed level of consumption will, therefore, be faster.

It is also conceivable that the increase in productivity brought about by the new technique adopted will not be the same in industry I and industry A. However, the differences in productivity among different industries, when seen over a long period of time and originating from a large number of innovations, should not be permanent, nor should they influence one industry more than the others in a given direction. Also in this case, technical progress should be distributed in such a way that the differences in productivity will have a random effect on the different branches of production.

[28] G. E. Stigler (*Capital and Rates of Return*, p. 91) writes: "There are moderately strong relationships of this measure of progress [rise in output per unit of input] with investment . . . the relationship between this measure of progress and rates of return is equally strong, and rather less expected." Although at our level of abstraction this statistical result may not be decisive, it reinforces the contention that there are laws of efficiency with respect to technical progress linked to the rate of profits. In the text above these laws are considered as though they were well established; in fact, the study of this aspect of economics is still at a very rudimentary level.

[29] This possibility does not influence the relationship between sectors K and C; for this purpose, technical progress continues to be neutral.

When speaking of differences in productivity among superior techniques in different sectors, one is arguing either in terms of changes of ratios among physical quantities (and no problem arises when this is the case) or in terms of changes of ratios among values (and there is no problem here until prices—in particular, the rate of profits—are given). In the present model, however, there is a process of differentiation of the rate of profits. Let us consider the ratio of productivities of technique 1 (in terms of units of investment) and of technique 2 in industry A on the one hand, and the ratio of productivities of techniques 3 and 4 in industry I on the other (techniques 2 and 4 being superior to techniques 1 and 3, respectively). A comparison between the two ratios loses its meaning if the rates of profits in the two industries are allowed to change independent of the change in productivity, since an independent variation of the profit rates will affect the value of investment, in terms of the units of investment in which the comparison between productivities in A and I is to be conducted.

This difficulty can be overcome if the comparison is made at rates of profits which differ but which are such that their ratios do not change. It is assumed, therefore, that the relative rates of profits for the existing commodities do not change in the period in which the comparison among productivities is undertaken. The resulting picture, however, is awkward: differences in productivity become neutral only over a long period of time, after a great number of innovations have produced a random pattern in technical progress. But the ability to recognize differences in productivities is only valid over a fairly short period; otherwise, changes in the consumption pattern will influence the rate of profits and thus blur the productivity picture. The purpose of my argument, on the other hand, is limited. The awkward picture is necessary only to indicate that if in the long run prices are determined by Engel's law, and relative prices change, the technical conditions of production will not inject an autonomous variation into the price pattern. No matter how this reasoning is stretched, it can be safely assumed that either neutrality will be assured in the long run or that whatever non-neutrality is created will work in the same direction as the law of development of consumption. In conclusion, the laws determining the changes in the structure of relative prices, the distribution of income as well as the preference scale of the economy, are not altered permanently by technology, and depend on other economic mechanisms.

5

THE DEVELOPMENT
OF CAPITALIST
PRODUCTION

Among the assumptions of the present model, the case of variable subsistence consumption was discussed. It was stated, in brief, that the growth process takes place, in the long run, through a continual increase in the quantity, and a continuous change in the type, of the commodities which make up the basic items of individual consumption.[1] This hypothesis, however, has not been incorporated into a complete, although simplified, description of the growth process.

If it is true that the profit motive and its parallel, the motive of maximum accumulation, are the psychological foundations of the process of production in a capitalist economy, there would seem to exist a contradiction between these motives and the increase of subsistence consumption in the long run. Entrepreneurs cannot increase wages and salaries without reducing the amount of capital that can be accumulated. On the other hand, they cannot prevent an increase in consumption in the face of increasing investment without reducing the realized rate of profits. If this contradiction were pushed to the limit and if it were possible to argue that the wage fund is fixed (in absolute terms if population is stationary, in relative terms if it increases), the capitalist system would break down. This is only one of the apparent contradictions which are discovered in the course of an interpretation of the growth process. It illustrates well our general problem, namely, the maintenance of a dynamic equilibrium in the capitalist system. In order to resolve this contradiction the workings of the system must be examined in some detail. In what follows, the rate or rates of profits stand for the "average" rate of profits of the economy.

ACCUMULATION AND TECHNICAL PROGRESS[2]

Let us start with a system in which there is no technical progress, population does not increase, and there is full employment. En-

---

[1] The role of new commodities is examined below, p. 122.

[2] This description is based on elements similar, although not identical, to

trepreneurs must invest all their profits, composed of the surplus derived from sector C. Sector K, therefore, will produce plants for sector C, but since full employment conditions prevail, the new productive capacity cannot be utilized. The profit that gave rise to the original investment cannot be further realized. If sector C increases money wages, sector K can release labor to sector C because in the absence of a realized profit that could be reinvested sector K will need less labor. Sector C, with this new labor force, can utilize a part of its new productive capacity. The volume of sales of consumer goods can rise because money wages have risen. A realized profit is created, although it will be smaller than it would under less than full employment conditions. Investment in the next period will thus be lower. Since full employment conditions continue to prevail, and since the new bout of investment will give sector C new plants which it cannot utilize unless labor is shifted from sector K and wages are increased again, the process is repeated. At the end of the process, sector K will be producing only replacements for worn-out plants;[3] the economy will not be growing; net profits, and therefore the rate of profits, will drop to zero; and wages will be absorbing the whole of net output. The system now faces a structural crisis which can be overcome only if technical progress is introduced.[4] Technical progress, by increasing output per man, frees manpower throughout the economy.

As a result, technical progress is also a means to overcome crises created by full employment conditions. The same volume of output

---

those contained in Mrs. Robinson's model. The reader who is unfamiliar with the questions dealt with in this chapter and who wishes to compare them with formalized analyses of Mrs. Robinson's model can have recourse to K. Lancaster, "Mrs. Robinson's Dynamics," *Economica* (February, 1960), and to R. Findlay, "The Robinson Model of Accumulation," *ibid.* (February, 1963).

[3] This will happen whether or not sectors K and C are identifiable in the real world. However, it seems reasonable that, where technical progress does not exist and the system risks a crisis resembling that described above, entrepreneurs will stop competing with each other in respect to wage rates and will avoid the progressive reduction of sector K and of the rate of profits. This crisis should be one of those which the class is able to cope with. If the class should succeed in creating monetary resources (by means of credit activities, government intervention, etc.) to be allocated to sector K as a substitute for profits which were not realized and also to permit an increase in money wages in that sector, sector C would not increase at the expense of sector K, and the crisis would become purely inflationary.

[4] If unemployment is present, in the absence of technical progress the increase in productive capacity will absorb the unemployed labor force, and the crisis will be delayed until full employment conditions are created.

in the economy, after new techniques are introduced, requires a smaller labor force. The reduction in the required labor force for a given output will permit the utilization of the new productive capacity without affecting sector K. Full employment conditions tend to be re-created.

WEAK ACCUMULATION

In our model, entrepreneurs save and invest all their income, which is composed exclusively of profits. The rate of accumulation permitted by technical progress is always sufficient to maintain full employment. If entrepreneurial consumption is taken as variable, then the rate of accumulation can become insufficient, and full employment may not be maintained. With technical progress and the rise of output per man, entrepreneurs can decide to consume the whole or part of the increased income originating from the increase in productivity. This may have a negative effect on the investment rate, and so-called "technological" unemployment may ensue. Unemployment will be accompanied by a reduction in the total wage bill in the economy, and the lower consumption of wage earners will result in a reduction in the volume of sales.

Total consumption and total sales will fail to decline only if the increased consumption of entrepreneurs exactly matches the reduction in the consumption of wage earners. Aside from the fact that consumption levels do not change rapidly, such a compensatory effect of entrepreneurs' consumption can only occur if the commodity composition of the additional consumption of entrepreneurs is the same as the composition of that part of consumption lost by wage earners. It is well known, however, that the consumption pattern changes with a change in income class. The required compensatory effect does not arise. Consequently, the structure of production would have to change in proportion to the change in the structure of consumption originating from the increased consumption of entrepreneurs, and this would cause a complete revolution in the productive system. On the other hand, rather than consume part of their additional income, entrepreneurs may hoard it.

Of course, any combination of these possibilities can occur. The consequences, as can easily be seen, are various and are not necessarily consistent with the maintenance of equilibrium. However, the case of weak accumulation can be easily overemphasized. I think that, although a possibility, weak accumulation is probably quite irrelevant as a factor in the capitalist system. There is no denying the fact that instances of weak accumulation are an every-day occurrence in developing countries. In fact, this phenomenon should be typical of economies in which capitalist production is still at a primitive stage, the accumulation and profit motives do not play a major role, and the capitalist-entrepreneur is absent or not sufficiently in control of the productive system. On the other hand, to admit that accumulation can be insufficient in a capitalist economy is probably contradictory. It would imply that the maxi-mum accumulation motive does not operate fully and that entrepre-neurs will cease to fulfill their primary task. In any case, our model admits entrepreneurial awareness of macroeconomic magnitudes, and this awareness—as indicated above—becomes operative when-ever the system approaches a crisis. Even without recourse to this hypothesis, however, a few observations on the choices open to entrepreneurs may clarify the modest role which weak accumula-tion can in fact play.

If monetary aspects were not excluded from our model, what would be the relevance of entrepreneurial hoarding of resources or, in other words, what would be the importance of liquidity preference? The decision to hoard is not a final one, like the deci-sion to consume or to invest. The phenomenon derives from en-trepreneurial expectations with regard to prices and profits: only as a result of certain profit rates which may or may not be obtained will entrepreneurs prefer to keep their surplus in liquid form. But whatever the level of the rate of profits which represents the point of indifference between the decision to invest and the decision to hoard, over a long period of time, if the rate of profits is con-sistently expected to be at a level lower than the indifference point, entrepreneurs will cease to hoard and will start to invest, since the tendency toward profit maximization is still present. One could object that the indifference point between decisions to invest and decisions to hoard could decline to a lower level than that indicated by the valuation of risk (or of any other motive for preferring re-sources in liquid form), *thus abolishing the profit motive.* However, as hoarding is undertaken precisely because risk is subject to a certain valuation, that indifference point cannot, by definition, be lower than the risk valuation.

If hoarding is excluded as a possible alternate entrepreneurial behavior which could lead, in the long run, to weak accumulation, then a judgment on the case of weak accumulation rests only on the importance that changes in entrepreneurial consumption can have in the capitalist system. There are reasons to believe that a variation in the absolute level of entrepreneurial consumption cannot reach proportions which would constitute a danger to the whole economy. First, it should be possible to apply to entrepreneurial consumption Keynes's "fundamental psychological law,"[5] according to which the propensity to save increases or remains constant with a rise in income.[6] Even more important is the fact that savings, as a source of investment within the entrepreneurial class, are not created in significant amounts at the level of family budgets but originate mainly from enterprises themselves,[7] and variations in the consumption of enterprises have, of course, little meaning per se in the long-run model (structurally they depend upon the character of technical progress). Mrs. Robinson, who makes the "thriftiness condition" a central behavioral variable in comparing different economies, observes that "the entrepreneurial aspect of capital is dominant and profit is desired mainly as a means of accumulating capital, rather than capital being desired mainly as a means of consuming profit. It is hard to believe that if the rentier aspect of capitalism had been dominant . . . the system would have . . . flourished so well as in fact has been the case."[8]

Had we admitted that workers can save, the picture would not be very different. Again, hoarding becomes irrelevant, since what was said about entrepreneurs can be applied, *mutatis mutandis*, to workers. As for consumption, this is entirely determined, in the long run, by the growth of wages and the resultant increase in the subsistence level of consumption. The problem of wages that rise too fast and weaken accumulation is better seen in the context of the discussion of excessive accumulation, since in the presence of technical progress the primary mover of wage rates is the entrepreneurial decision.

If hoarding is unimportant in the long run, and changes in consumption play only an insignificant role, even if an entrepreneurial behavior different, in terms of expectations, from the special "omnis-

[5] See Keynes, *General Theory*, p. 96.

[6] The "ratchet" effect (see p. 24 above) and the demonstration effect (see p. 119, n. 1, below) tend to confirm this behavior. Empirical investigations, in time series and in cross-section, have universally confirmed the hypothesis that the average propensity to save does not decrease with a rise in income and with a rise in income classes.

[7] See G. Fuá, *Lo stato e il risparmio privato* (Turin, 1961), pp. 141–44.

[8] *Accumulation of Capital*, p. 392.

cience" of the entrepreneurial class discussed above had been taken into account, an important place as a variable in our simplified model could not have been assigned to the investment function. There will, of course, be a relationship between investment, income, and profit rates in our model, but it becomes a secondary relationship, derived from, and overshadowed by, other relationships (such as that determining the increase in wages).[9]

The problem of weak accumulation and, in principle, that of excessive accumulation become relevant, however, when technical progress expresses itself in new techniques which require resources out of proportion to those actually available. This situation has been already dealt with in the description of the character of technical progress (see Chapter 4 above). It was concluded there that in the long run it was likely that new techniques would be neutral in character. The relevant assumption here is that the economy is closed. Were it open, the probability that new techniques are neutral would be reduced, and the equilibrium of the economy would be endangered (Appendix A briefly examines this question).

ACCUMULATION AND HISTORICAL INCREASE IN WAGES

Economic analysis, either from love of symmetry or, perhaps, as a result of historical visions which tend to universalize particular socioeconomic systems, has given equal importance to the case of weak accumulation and of excessive accumulation. From what was

[9] Keynes showed that decisions to save and to invest are made by different economic agents, and that savings and investment need not be equal (*ex ante*); as a result, there is no automatic mechanism between savings and investment. However, M. Kalecki (*Economic Dynamics*, pp. 54–56) has elegantly illustrated how investment finances itself, in the sense that it creates the savings which are necessary to cause it. By admitting that profits can be either consumed or hoarded, or that savings out of profits do not have an *ex ante* relationship with investment, a formidable problem was created regarding the determination, and the shape, of the investment function (or, as it has been also called, the investment demand function, or the schedule of the marginal efficiency of capital). Many solutions have been proposed. For example, R. F. Harrod ("Notes on the Trade Cycle," *Economic Journal* [June, 1952]) concludes that increases in output induce increases in the stock of capital necessary to yield that increase in output (the accelerator), which shifts the problem to the determination of consumption and of entrepreneurial expectations. Mrs. Robinson introduces the notion of innate entrepreneurial characteristics ("animal spirits") sustained by a particular assumption regarding their expectations and the way in which they evaluate capital. Kaldor links the investment function to the rate of technical progress. For the reasons indicated in the text this subject has not been touched upon here.

said above, it would seem that excessive accumulation merits the most attention.

Let us return to the assumption that entrepreneurs do not consume. The introduction of technical progress and the increase in output per man allow the continuous increase in productive capacity to be utilized. In this case, unemployment is not created, but the total output of the economy increases. If wages do not rise, or if they do not rise in proportion to the increase in output per man —and this is a realistic possibility because of the motive of maximum accumulation—total consumption will not rise, or will not rise in proportion to the increase in productive capacity, and the additional output (or part of it) will not be sold.[10] The rate of profits which entrepreneurs look forward to as a result of the adoption of technical progress will not be realized. With the prospect of a stagnation of sales, prices of commodities will decrease and real wages and sales will again increase; but because the market structure is monopolistic, a general reduction of the price level must be excluded.[11] If monopolists, in these conditions, do not raise money wages, and since prices do not decrease, the economy will be spinning its wheels. Technical progress will cause a steady increase in output per man, investment will continue, productive capacity will increase, and the additional production will remain unsold. The faster technical progress is adopted, the greater the unused productive capacity and the reduction of the profit rate will be. The system will thus enter a cumulative crisis (called a crisis of underconsumption).[12]

---

[10] Almost all models show the contradiction between an increase in wages and the profit motive, but very few try to solve it. Kaldor, for example, has criticized Marx for having failed to predict correctly the increase in real wages in capitalist economies but does not explain why or how it came about. Mrs. Robinson has recourse to the humanitarian instincts of entrepreneurs and their *savoir-faire*, which do not seem strong bases for explaining a fundamental feature of the system.

[11] It is well known that the presence of monopolistic concentrations means (1) that new entrepreneurs will not be able to enter the sectors where profits are higher, therefore preventing a reduction in prices; and (2) that monopolists can increase prices (or avoid reducing them) without seriously affecting their sales in favor of possible rivals.

[12] A school of thought which considers this aspect of underconsumption a cause of the crisis of the capitalist system is that of Marxian origin. According to O. Bauer and P. M. Sweezy (see the latter's *Capitalist Development*, Appendix to chap. X), the economy will face a fundamental contradiction, when it grows at constant or decreasing rates, between the growth of investment as dictated by the profit motive and the growth of investment deriving from the increase in consumption. A serious discussion followed the statement

If entrepreneurs do not increase wages with the rise of output per man, they will succeed in avoiding a crisis only if they introduce new superior techniques that will not result in increasing output of consumer goods—for example, if technical progress is introduced only in the sector producing investment goods. A process of "complication" of the productive structure will result, through which technical progress will increase the efficiency of machines producing other machines, but not the efficiency of machines producing for consumption. The increase in productive capacity, necessary in order to employ the manpower freed by technical progress, will expand the chain of production through the further mechanization of the different stages of production in the sector producing investment goods.

Such a process, insofar as it depends on the initiative of entrepreneurs, is clearly absurd. Even if it were possible, technically, to "complicate" the productive structure, it would also be necessary to limit technical progress to one sector exclusively (or, more appropriately, to those industries which do not produce for final consumption). In such a case, technical progress would not be neutral; and after what was said regarding the character of new techniques and, in particular, regarding the impossibility of identifying sectors K and C in the real world, that mechanism cannot exist. The system would never have been born if it had had to be based on technical progress limited to the investment goods sector.[13]

It would also be absurd to claim that entrepreneurs do not know that they cannot dispose of the social surplus without causing the producers of the surplus, the wage earners, to claim it for themselves. The presence of different economic civilizations, like the Communist one, is a direct challenge to a system which bases itself on fixed real wage rates. In fact, the real wage rate has increased in capitalist economies.[14] Entrepreneurs, then, know that the capi-

---

of this theory (see, among the more recent contributions, N. Georgescu-Roegen, "Mathematical Proofs of the Breakdown of Capitalism," *Econometrica* [April, 1960]). Whether or not this theory proves the existence of a destructive (dialectic) contradiction of the system, it does point out the importance of this contradiction.

[13] One should not forget that capitalism was not born in a political and social vacuum; on the contrary, it had to fight older economic systems and, from the start, had to prove its greater efficiency.

[14] It is necessary to spend a few words on the concept of "increase" or "stagnation" of wages. Within the definition of a measure of value used here, there is no doubt that wages have risen. However, this is a weak basis (at least philosophically) from which to criticize Marx's law of progressive

talist system cannot but produce for consumption, even though their own goal is maximum accumulation. The determination of whether this knowledge is an effect of learning or a natural tendency of capitalist societies is a problem for historians (we shall discuss an aspect of this problem later[15]).

Because the market structure is monopolistic, and because monopolies are the foundation of the self-awareness of the entrepreneurial class, in that they allow entrepreneurs to calculate the effects of their decisions on the economy as a whole, entrepreneurs know that without increasing wages along with the increase in output per man, they will not be capable of utilizing investment and will risk a reduction in their profit rate. They have a choice between setting up "realization crises" and simply permitting real wages to increase. Such crises have been described in the economic literature,[16] and it does not seem useful to analyze their essential characteristics here. In today's world, in particular since the second world war, entrepreneurs seem to have encouraged an increase in real wages (perhaps under the stimulus of the different civilizations mentioned above). While the realization crises were resolved by the use of political tools (such as government intervention in the economy), the increase in real wages has occurred through a new co-operation between entrepreneurs and trade unions.[17] In this con-

---

pauperization. Since the value of the different mixes of commodities making up the wage bill in different time periods has meaning only if it is referred to a social complex of aims—in this model, the complex of aims of the entrepreneurial class—it may well be that what seems an increase in real wages from the viewpoint of entrepreneurs is, from the viewpoint of workers, an objective pauperization. Even more to the point, what may seem today an increase in real wages from "everybody's" point of view, tomorrow can be considered pauperization in relation to the general complex of aims valid at that time. This is a logic, however, from which an economist is excluded.

[15] See below, p. 102.

[16] See Sweezy, *Capitalist Development*, chaps. viii–xii.

[17] Trade unions are probably a principal means through which the capitalist system can survive. The existence of trade unions, which push continuously for wage increases and which, in their most advanced forms, are no less efficiently organized than industrial corporations, prevents the individual entrepreneur, with his possible "selfishness" in the short run, from forcing wages down or preventing their rise. In spite of this, however, trade unions do not really possess an autonomy of decision within the capitalist system, since they have no part in the control of consumption (and, therefore, in the control of production, in the long run). Unions are thus a force at the service of the system, in constant tension: without being a part of the entrepreneurial class, they permit the latter to express itself in informal, rather than formal, control organs and to avoid crises which arise from insufficient wage increases.

text, it is worth observing that the self-awareness of the class must, historically, have developed along with the economic system and that it should today be considerably more complete than it was, say, at the time of the Industrial Revolution.

Those Marxian economists (Rosa Luxemburg, for example) who regarded the contradiction between the accumulation motive and the need to increase wages as the cause of a quick liquidation of capitalism had an excessively restrictive vision of the system. In fact, if the class is self-aware there is no contradiction. The maximum profit and maximum accumulation motives continue to be the springboards of capitalist production, but when faced with the possibility of structural crises which endanger the very existence of the system, the class is capable—and it is obvious that it should be so—of forcing its members to increase wages. The more monopolistic production is and the tighter the class is, the smoother the process is: entrepreneurs already know that growth and rising wages go together. The fact that wages increase continually derives from the empirical knowledge of entrepreneurs that allowing wages to increase—in the face of technical progress—does not decrease the profit rate and the rate of accumulation, does not affect the main characteristics of the system, and only reinforces the dominant position of their class. The apparent contradiction between the accumulation motive and the increase in real wages is thus solved by recourse to entrepreneurial class consciousness and the control that the class has over the development of the economy.

As an example, let us suppose that the bargaining power of entrepreneurs vis-à-vis wage earners is, for some reason, weakened to the point where money wages increase more rapidly than the increase in output per man—a situation that, at first glance, would seem to lead to a situation of weak accumulation. Since entrepreneurs control production and investment, and since a reduction in the rate of profits and in the share of profits in the economy's net output deriving from an increase in wages larger than the increase in productivity is not, by definition, acceptable to entrepreneurs, the increase in money wages will be transformed into rising prices and inflationary pressures. In the real world, where wage earners are above all consumers and possess an insignificant share of the "owned" means of production, inflation represents the principal way in which the entrepreneurial class keeps income distribution in line with the fruits of technical progress. Inflation could be avoided only if the whole of the increase in wages in excess of the increase in productivity could be transferred to savings and investment. Since this can come about only if the wage earners' share of the means of production increases, the class could not permit it without reneging on its own function. An inflationary crisis is perhaps the simplest form of political and social intervention of the class; it cannot be solved other than by means of economic policy. And since inflation hits all income classes, the measures adopted by the entrepreneurial class to reduce or eliminate it are among those least dependent on the dialectics of opposing classes.

The process by which real wages increase must be a continuous one; the necessity to allow wages to rise in relation to an actual or potential accumulative excess can always be repeated. Moreover, once wages have been allowed to rise, it is hard to imagine that they can remain stagnant, since the stimulus to increase wages is for workers what the profit motive is for entrepreneurs. In reality it may well happen that after entrepreneurs have allowed wages to rise, and are confronting a reduction (albeit potential) of profit rates, they may then try to reduce wages. However, in the long run the subsistence level of consumption will rise. Entrepreneurs thus could not reduce real wages below the level of psychological subsistence without reducing the productivity of labor, and the increase in real wages becomes irreversible in the long run.

I have already mentioned, in speaking of weak accumulation, that the character of new techniques and of accumulation are not independent of each other. Accumulation can be excessive if technical progress has a labor-using (capital-saving) bias. When an isolated economy is considered, there is little likelihood of excessive accumulation taking place. But when an open economy is considered (see Appendix A), there is a real problem, and the equilibrium of the economy is not assured.

TECHNICAL PROGRESS AND PROFITS

How do profits, accumulation, and technical progress play their respective roles in the growth of the system? Let us imagine a situation in which initially there was unemployment, and entrepreneurs obtained a profit from the production process. Investment will go on, in the absence of technical progress, until all unemployment has been absorbed. Even if technical progress (of a neutral character) is introduced, the process by which unemployment is reabsorbed is not interrupted. What follows explains why this is so and provides another reason why technical progress is a necessary condition for the maintenance of the system's equilibrium.

Let us suppose that the economy is in full employment and technical progress is absent. Profits already realized are invested, but investment cannot be utilized, and the economy is risking a progressive annihilation of sector K and a structural crisis (see above, p. 94). We now take technical progress into account, however, and assume that it increases productivity, leaving total output unchanged. To simplify, we also assume that technical progress consists of improvements that can be directly applied to existing plants. These innovations, by increasing output per head, release a supply of labor. The additional productive capacity of sector C, resulting from previously invested profits, can now be utilized. Profits, in turn, can be realized, sector K does not decline, and the rate of profits does not tend toward zero. On the other hand, technical progress represents a saving of production costs for entrepreneurs and gives rise to a new and autonomous profit which equals the amount of wages which would have been paid by entrepreneurs to the labor force now released by technical progress. If this new profit could be readily invested, it would absorb, by definition, all the labor force released by technical progress. But this labor—wholly or in part—has already been utilized by sector C in the productive capacity created by investing the profits which had been obtained previously. The system, therefore, generates an amount of profit[18] which, although it could create new productive capacity, cannot be realized because full employment conditions have already been attained. A new crisis looms on the horizon, and only new technical progress can prevent it.

Two observations can be derived from this description. First, we can confirm that the non-realized amount of profits makes it necessary that technical progress be continuously introduced in the economy: technical progress itself generates an amount of profit that is not realized, thus assuring the presence of an automatic incentive for its introduction. Second, if there is unemployment to begin with, there is no difficulty in realizing that amount of profit —wholly or in part—even in the presence of technical progress.

In conclusion, the total realized profit in conditions of full em-

---

[18] This amount equals the profit realized previously minus the sum of the savings derived from technical progress and of the profit realized by means of the utilization of the labor force freed by technical progress (namely, the increase in output per man).

ployment depends on technical progress and will be proportional to the increase in output per man. The "average" rate of profit will remain constant each time the process described above is completed; investment, too will be proportional to the increase in output per man.[19]

EQUILIBRIUM AND THE DEVELOPMENT OF THE SYSTEM

It is now possible to summarize briefly the mode of development of the economy. Full employment conditions prevail. If entrepreneurs obtain a profit from production, they must invest it, but the rise in productive capacity cannot be utilized, by virtue of full employment; entrepreneurs will continuously adopt technical progress; technical progress increases output per man, releases labor, permits the utilization of productive capacity, and re-creates conditions of full employment; the rate of profits, however, will decline if the increased output resulting from the increased productive capacity is not sold; real wages must rise; the adoption of technical progress, which releases labor, permits the utilization of productive capacity and realizes the profit obtained previously, but does not also permit the full utilization of the productive capacity which technical progress itself created by means of an increase in profits; and since full employment conditions are re-created, entrepreneurs cannot but opt for technical progress again.

The different stages of this process occur mainly in the short run, as defined here. The results of the whole process, in the long run, will be as follows:

1. the "average" level of the profit rate will tend to remain constant;

---

[19] Scientific-technical research, a necessary condition of technical progress, becomes also a necessary condition of economic growth. This research has been treated here as though it were carried on continuously. However, it may not be carried on continuously, or it may not yield new technologies continuously; and the consequences of these possible malfunctions are disastrous: because full employment conditions prevail, *ex hypothesi*, new investment in "old" techniques is not utilized, the economy stagnates, and the profit rate tends toward zero. Mrs. Robinson calls this a position of economic "bliss," but in fact it is a complete negation of the system. However, such a possibility does not seem realistic, at least within the framework of our model, since the tendency towards maximum profits, maximum accumulation, and maximum technical progress constitutes the foundation of the capitalist system. Also, we have observed that there exists an automatic incentive for the introduction (and therefore research) of new techniques.

2. the real wage rate will increase either through an increase in money wages or through a reduction in consumer goods prices;[20]

3. the relative size of the different productive sectors of the economy will not change as a result of this process; in other words, sectors C and K will not change in relation to each other;

4. the relative shares in total output of profits and wages—as well as of investment and consumption—will tend to remain constant; and

5. the marginal capital-output ratio will tend to remain constant, while the capital-labor ratio will increase in proportion to the increase in output per man.

If the capital-output ratio and the relative shares of wages and profits in output remain constant; if we could picture the rate of profits for the economy as a whole; and if the problem of measuring values is solvable according to our hypothesis, then the rate of growth of income and output will be equal or proportional to the rate of profits.[21]

In the long run, the increase in the subsistence wage determines (whether it is the sole determinant or not is irrelevant) the introduction of technical progress and thus the increase in output per

---

[20] As was already noted, the existence of monopolies makes the rise in money wages more likely.

[21] We arrive thus at a "post-Keynesian" formulation of equilibrium. The equality or the proportionality of the rate of profits and the rate of growth of the economy can be expressed in the following manner (see N. Kaldor, "Alternative Theories"):

$$\frac{P}{K} = \frac{I}{K}$$

(if capitalists do not consume and workers do not save), where P = profits, K = quantity of capital, and I = investment. Since the increase in output is a function of investment, $DY = aI$, where a represents the incremental capital-output ratio, and

$$\frac{DY}{Y} = \frac{aI}{Y}, \quad \text{or} \quad \frac{I}{Y} = \frac{1}{a} \frac{DY}{Y};$$

and since the rate of profits can be expressed as

$$\frac{P}{K} = \frac{I}{K} = \frac{I}{Y} \frac{Y}{K};$$

and since $Y = bK$, where b represents the (average) capital-output ratio; and since in equilibrium a = constant and $a = b$; then

$$\frac{P}{K} = \frac{bI}{Y} = \frac{b}{a} \frac{DY}{Y} = \frac{DY}{Y},$$

which illustrates the relationship between the rate of profits and the rate of growth in equilibrium. J. Von Neumann ("General Economic Equilibrium") had already pioneered in obtaining this result: "the interest factor and the coefficient of expansion of the economy are equal and uniquely determined by the technically possible processes. . . ."

man. This increase causes total output to rise, since it re-creates full employment conditions, and determines a new level of profits and of investment (the rate of accumulation). The introduction of technical progress, then, controls the rate of growth of the economy. The rate of accumulation and the "average" rate of profits are determined by the growth rate, given the marginal capital-output ratio, which, in turn, depends on the character of technical progress. The profit-income ratio, investment-output ratio, and distribution of income are determined by the rate of profits, given the capital-output ratio.[22]

Let us observe, in passing, that even though the relative size of sectors K and C does not change, the size of the different industries within sectors K and C can—and usually will—change as a result of Engel's law, without affecting the results described above.

In conclusion, the various forces working at cross-purposes in the real world will balance each other out, principally as a result of the self-awareness of the entrepreneurial class and its ability to act as the regulator of the system and of the probability that technical progress will take on a neutral character. Under these conditions, the rate of growth of the economy depends on the rate at which technical progress is adopted. The latter, in the long run,

---

[22] In the neoclassical model, the existence of a series of alternative techniques of production is not necessarily in contrast with this formulation. The rate of profits, determined by the rate of growth of the economy, which depends in turn upon technical progress, given the propensities to save and consume of the two classes, permits the choice of the optimum technique, which in turn determines the capital-output ratio (see L. Pasinetti, "Rate of Profits and Income Distribution in Relation to the Rate of Economic Growth," *Review of Economic Studies* [October, 1962]). In our model only one technique is available; even putting aside the argument given in Chapter 4 above, there are other reasons to exclude multiple alternative techniques from long-run analyses. The longer the time necessary to put them into operation, the less relevant they are. Let us suppose that we are in full employment conditions. To avoid a crisis of the type described on p. 94, and in the presence of alternative techniques, entrepreneurs will try to adopt those techniques with the highest degree of mechanization. Aside from the fact that such techniques may not be available (for reasons of technological discontinuities), the longer is the time necessary to adopt them, the more likely it is that new, superior techniques will become available in the interim; and when technical progress occurs there is no need to resort to the older mechanized techniques. Moreover, the more mechanized techniques must be such as to yield a higher rate of profits than the technique to be abandoned, *after calculating as an additional cost the discounted profits that the old plant can still yield.* The likelihood that techniques of production of the more mechanized type can in fact be chosen in these circumstances without being confused with superior techniques seems very small.

depends (although not solely) on the rate of increase in the sub-sistence level of consumption, or on the rate of transformation of consumption into subsistence consumption.[23]

There remains one last point to clarify. This is not a so-called "endogenous" theory of growth. The new techniques may require a level of investment which is not compatible with other economic quantities, or the wage rate may not increase in step with the in-crease in output per man. There are good reasons to think that equilibrium will not be disturbed in a closed economy: we have talked of the neutral character of techniques and of entrepreneurial "omniscience." However, some of these factors do not appear to originate from within the mechanism of the capitalist system. In other words, the equilibrium of the capitalist system does not simply *occur:* it is *created* in the course of the historical develop-ment of the system. Appendix A will show that, once the economy is open, each individual economy may not be in equilibrium. How-ever, disequilibrium in one economy does not imply disequilibrium for all the economies. The international capitalist system is not necessarily unstable.

A note before closing this discussion. Up to now I have spoken of the increase in the productive capacity of the economy as an increase in the capacity of existing plants producing the complex of commodities consumed at any given moment. However, following Engel's law and its logical implications, the increase in productive capacity for the economy as a whole must be seen also as (1) the new production of commodities not previously existing and (2) the increase in the production of certain goods at a faster rate than the production of other goods. As was observed above, these three aspects of the increase in productive capacity may be aggregated and considered as an increase of the capacity of the economy as a whole only by having recourse to a measure with historical-social characteristics which reflect the order of preferences of the entre-preneurial class.

WAGES AND THE WAGE RATE

It is interesting to illustrate briefly the role of wages in the de-velopment mechanism of capitalism. Class consciousness and the

[23] I am not talking in terms of comparative statics: therefore, the initial levels of the rate of profit and of wages are not relevant.

presence of trade unions make it possible for the system to register a constant upward push in money wages. Without technical progress the wage push would result in inflation; but because the tendency to obtain technical progress is always present—it is of the same nature as the tendency to maximize profits—in the long run the money wage push will be satisfied in real terms. Through the steps indicated in the previous pages, real wages will continually increase in proportion to the rate of growth of output per man. Therefore, a long-run linear relationship between wage increases and technical progress can be established.

Since in the long run the increase in wages is transformed into an increase in the subsistence level, the increase in the psychological substance level is also continual. Given a certain increase in wages, its transformation into a higher subsistence level will require a certain time. It seems evident, therefore, that in the long run the subsistence level of wages will expand at the rate at which wages rise, and that it will be equal to, or less than, the current level of wages at any given moment. The gap which is thus created is subject to fluctuations, in the short run, depending upon the capacity of entrepreneurs to change the level of wages. On the other hand, we have noted that the shares of profits and of wages—insofar as the latter exceed the subsistence level and cease to be part of the means of production—tend to remain constant. Real wages, of course, cannot decline below the level of psychological subsistence without generating a crisis in the economy. The rate of accumulation and the increase in real wages—permitted and sustained by the self-awareness of the entrepreneurial class—as well as the rise in the subsistence level of wages are thus a function of technical progress.

Parallel to the process of differentiation of profit rates, a process of differentiation of wage rates can be conceived. It is well known that the more monopolistic an enterprise is, the less its inhibitions about increasing money wages are, not only because of its better knowledge of the economy as a whole but also because of its fear of new competitors. Moreover, trade unions are better organized in such enterprises and enjoy a stronger bargaining power. Since the more monopolistic enterprises are also those which have a higher rate of profits, the fact that the wage rate paid by them tends to be higher than the wage rate paid by less monopolistic enterprises has an influence on the working of Engel's law in favor of their own products.[24] This observation confirms, in a more indirect way, the statement that wages are not an original factor of capitalist growth, but depend on the choices and on the behavior of entrepreneurs. In any event, the differentiation in wage rates is not in contrast with the differentiation of profit rates, which remains necessary whatever the level of wages and however they are differentiated.[25]

ACCUMULATION, TECHNICAL PROGRESS, AND THE DIFFERENTIATION OF PROFIT RATES

In our model consumption of different commodities increases at different rates of growth. This creates a differentiated structure of profit rates and causes or justifies the formation of monopolies. It was said that the productive system need not everywhere present the same degree of monopoly. Certain industries, the consumption of whose commodities increases less rapidly, may find themselves in a competitive market. The closer one approaches conditions of free competition, the more likely it is that prices of commodities will decrease and real wages increase in conditions of underconsumption. Let us examine some consequences of this possible asymmetry.

Money wages are, *ex hypothesi*, uniform throughout the economy. In the presence of underconsumption conditions, when the less monopolistic enterprises reduce their prices, real wages increase. If prices of more monopolistic enterprises do not decrease, the consumption of the commodities produced by less monopolistic enterprises tend to rise at a faster rate. This could upset the existing structure of profit rates. However, in the long run—and this question will arise again later on—whatever the behavior of prices, Engel's law must continue to be valid. Thus, the price reduction of commodities the consumption of which was already increasing at a lesser rate will make this consumption grow faster than it otherwise would *only for a short time*; the reduction will permit consumers to satisfy faster their need for this type of commodity. Actually, this consumption may not increase at all. Since the price reduction corresponds to an increase in disposable income of consumers, they will tend to direct their additional income towards

[24] This effect has been discussed by L. Spaventa, "Dualism in Economic Growth," *Banca Nazionale del Lavoro Quarterly Review* (December, 1959).

[25] In other words, prices will be such as to absorb the difference in wages and still maintain a higher profit rate for the industry which grows faster.

the consumption of commodities which satisfy the properties of Engel's law.[26] In conclusion, price changes arising from the structure of the market do not have enough influence to modify the basic tendencies of consumption. In fact, the former derive from the latter, in my model.

When, in the face of full employment conditions, money wages increase, the more monopolistic entrepreneurs allow them to rise with greater ease. Thus the increase in money wages will not occur uniformly in all industries. The price structure, therefore, will change and the relative prices of less monopolistic industries will be reduced. A result similar to that described above is obtained.

Let us examine now, in more general terms, how the differentiation of profit rates can be integrated into the development process. We start from a simple biological subsistence level of wages. Since consumption is, by definition, stationary, the rate of profits is uniform throughout the economy. This is the primitive stage of capitalism, in which the market structure is nearest to the conditions of free competition. Entrepreneurs, who obtain a profit from production, proceed to accumulate and adopt new, superior techniques; and for the purpose of realizing the maximum potential profit, they are obliged to increase wages beyond the biological subsistence level. This is the first and fundamental realization crisis, the act of birth of the capitalist system. Since the market structure is near to free competition, the class has not yet acquired self-awareness. Unless other factors are introduced, individual entrepreneurs may well be unable to avoid maintaining wages at their subsistence level. The system, as a result, will spin into a crisis, and the full development of capitalist production will be interrupted.[27] This is the

[26] This is the income effect of a price change (see J. R. Hicks, *Value and Capital* [Oxford, 1939], p. 32). Given the general level of my analysis, it may perhaps be useful to note that in cases such as that described in the text above my model greatly reduces the importance of the other effect on demand of a price change: the substitution effect. This effect, in the long run, clashes with the law of graduation of needs. If, for example, consumers have exceeded the psychological subsistence level of consumption, and if the price of a commodity included within that level declines, there is no substitution effect for that commodity. Hicks, on the contrary, states that only the latter effect is certain, while the income effect is far less likely. He deals with static equilibrium, but even when he examines dynamic aspects (*Value and Capital*, p. 231), he does not discuss this phenomenon.

[27] Even if there were no class awareness from an economic point of view, one could suppose the existence of a class consciousness from a political or social point of view, if this assumption did not raise the equally difficult problem of the origin of a political or social awareness. It is more reasonable to

initial contradiction of capitalism. The system, in fact, had to create its own "rules of the game" by revolution, in order to survive. On the other hand, history has shown a number of economies which have not been able to overcome this hurdle. It is perhaps the realization of the difficulties of this initial step which has pushed many less developed countries to try and substitute government intervention for the entrepreneurial class in economic activity.

Once the difficult birth is over, the growth process described above becomes continuous (even if it happens at discrete intervals, and through occasional crises). In the long run, the subsistence level of consumption rises. Consumption does not rise proportionately in all its components, and the consumption of certain commodities will increase at a faster rate than that of others. The need to produce certain commodities faster than others induces, through the observed mechanism, a differentiation of profit rates. This is not in contradiction with the profit maximization motive because Engel's law is a structural feature of all economic systems and must, therefore, create those dividing lines which make possible the differentiation. The profit motive will thus be valid within each class of profits. The differentiation of profit rates creates or justifies the existence of monopolistic forms which, in turn, help to maintain the differentiation. Monopolies increase the degree of self-awareness of the entrepreneurial class and ensure that the system is capable of maintaining itself by means of the continuous rise in real wages permitted by technical progress.

NEW COMMODITIES AND CAPITALIST DEVELOPMENT

When consumption increases in the long run, new commodities must be introduced in the economy so as to satisfy Engel's law. If a new commodity requires, for its own production, an amount of resources greater than what current investment allows, or greater than the amount necessary for the production of the commodity the additional consumption of which is replaced by the new commodity, there would result a case of temporary "complication" of the productive structure, and the investment rate (assuming that technical progress is present) increases: sector K would

---

suppose that the period of formation of the entrepreneurial-capitalist class—a period when competitive conditions should logically be strongest—has occurred when the scene was still dominated by systems (like the feudal one) which would not demonstrate that greater degree of competition.

thus grow in relation to sector C. Entrepreneurs, when technical progress is present, could, therefore, avoid increasing wages in order to obtain the necessary increase in the rate of investment. We are interested in the final result of this process. Although there has been a pause in wage increases, the new commodity will eventually have to be sold, and the wage rate will eventually have to increase anew. When the commodity is sold, sector K will have increased permanently in relation to sector C, and the share of wages —insofar as they exceed the subsistence level—on net income will have decreased. This possibility would imply a structural "jump" in the equilibrium of the system, but its significance is doubtful. There is no general law according to which a new commodity should have a capital-using or a capital-saving bias in relation to the commodity the additional consumption of which it is replacing. If this is true, and if the number of new commodities introduced into the economy (including the changes in existing commodities) is large, in the long run there should be a law of neutrality regarding the influence that new commodities have on the equilibrium of the system.[28]

The problem of those less developed economies which want to minimize the time span necessary to achieve a "modern" structure of consumption is different. The levels of wages and consumption must forcibly be kept low for the purpose of obtaining a rate of accumulation sufficient to build, in a short time period, a productive structure comparable to that of more advanced economies. This policy, as it interferes with the increase in real wages, changes the relative proportions of the sectors producing investment goods and consumer goods. The system of values and of relative prices will change in relation to that which is applicable to an advanced capitalist economy.

In a capitalist economy, therefore, the change in the structure of consumption deriving from the introduction of new commodities is one of the causes of the differentiation of profit rates. The introduction of new commodities, in the long run, will not affect the proportion of sectors K and C so much as it will change the prevalent structure of profit rates, while the "average" rate of profits would not necessarily be affected. The introduction of new com-

[28] It is not suggested here that any commodity is always compatible with the capitalist productive system. See, on this subject, Chapter 6 below, pp. 127–29.

modities can thus be treated in the same way as the change in the composition of consumption of already existing commodities.

It seems worth while, at the cost of a brief digression, to observe the relationship existing between the development of consumption and the change in the structure of production. It has been maintained that the most efficient path—in terms of output—between two positions having different compositions of consumption is that which, most of the way, runs close (as illustrated by Von Neumann) to that path in which there is proportional growth of all the activities composing the productive system, and diverges from the path of proportional growth only at the end. If this observation— the so-called turnpike theorem[29]—is true, capitalist development, which occurs through a continuous change in the composition of produced and consumed commodities, is not "optimum." The discussion on this question, on the other hand, is far from being at an end. Let us note, for example, that both Von Neumann's model and the elaboration of the turnpike theorem are based on a pure and perfect competition model, as one of the conditions of the linearity of the system of equations. But the competitive model is incompatible with a disproportionate growth of the sectors. It becomes a petition of principle, therefore, to define as optimum that path which is nearest to that of pure and perfect competition.

MONOPOLIES AND CAPITALIST DEVELOPMENT

An important consequence of the introduction of new commodities and, in general, of the development of consumption according to Engel's law is that the monopolies which are present at each moment (unless it is the monopolists themselves who determine Engel's law, a postulate which will be examined and rejected in the next chapter) may change in the long run according to the choices made by consumers. Monopolists, therefore, could engage in a struggle among themselves to avoid a decline in the rate of profits attributable to each of them and to claim for themselves the production of that commodity whose consumption is growing fastest. The monopolistic structure would therefore be very "fragile," although, given the length of our long period, it would still be much more durable than a monopolistic structure that depended only on

[29] First discussed by R. Dorfman, P. Samuelson, and R. M. Solow, *Linear Programming*, pp. 330–34. The authors state that "if origin and destination are far enough apart, it will always pay to get on the turnpike and cover distance at the best rate of travel, even if this means adding a little mileage at either end."

technological discontinuities. However, the simplest way in which the productive structure may change following a change in the structure of consumption is by a gradual adjustment of existing monopolies to the new conditions of consumption by means of a change of the product mix of the enterprise; in this way each enterprise tends to maintain its dominant position through time. Self-financing and the advantage, in terms of technical progress, which the more dynamic enterprises enjoy should also facilitate the conservation of enterprises as time goes on.[30]

Many economists have considered monopolistic concentrations more as obstacles than as positive elements in the process of capitalist development. In effect, the tendency of monopolies to keep prices stable in the presence of underconsumption conditions eliminates an automatic mechanism which could facilitate the orderly growth of the system. However, if it is true that this tendency eliminates an automatic re-equilibrating mechanism, it is also true that the presence of monopolies—the foundation of class awareness—remedies a series of other disequilibria and gives a rational basis to the movement of the system. Also, monopolies are able to separate the different production lines and permit a differentiated structure of profit rates, and, consequently, they are an essential means by which consumption is permitted to develop at different rates for different commodities.

In these pages monopolies have been characterized in a different way from that of many economists. They are not seen as entities caught in the narrow selfishness of the enterprise, attempting to increase profit margins even at the risk of explosive crises. In the long run, monopolies are seen here primarily as regulators of the development process because they provide entrepreneurs with that foresight which permits them to know, more or less approximately, the effect of their actions on the economy as a whole. Without monopolies, therefore, the capitalist form of economy would not exist.

THE ENTREPRENEURIAL CLASS

We have given considerable weight to the "class" aspect of entrepreneurs. This does not mean that the entrepreneurial class is to be looked upon as an aggregate that always expresses correctly the

[30] Monopolistic enterprises, in order to maintain themselves, must probably incur some special costs (public relations, political maneuvers, etc.). Either these costs are dealt with as production costs or they are part of the profits of the enterprise. I have not studied this aspect.

general will of its components. The description here is valid only in the long run, in which the struggle among entrepreneurs has already been resolved and in which only the main development trends stand out in sharp relief. In a shorter period, it is far from clear that the class is a homogeneous entity. A look at every-day economic reality will reveal the role which the differences among monopolists in one country, monopolists in different countries, and different countries each representing their strongest national monopolistic groups play in the development of capitalism. I am not interested, for the moment, in a detailed examination of these struggles. The process described above shows that capitalism cannot be conceived as a system in which the rationalizing principle is the play of demand and supply, regarded as independent forces. Smith's invisible hand does not exist. Once it is admitted that monopolists (capitalists, entrepreneurs) exercise a class function of the type I have described, their ability to determine the aims of the system certainly cannot be limited to the mere phenomenon of production. It seems obvious that not all consumer needs can be satisfied by commodities which invariably correspond—through the respective productive processes—to the type of economic society expressed or desired by capitalists. An example will suffice. Let us suppose that consumer tastes—once the biological subsistence level has been exceeded—have the capacity to focus autonomously on increased consumption of "education." This sector does not have a productive structure similar to that which is at the foundation of the capitalist system as it is known today. There is no factory production of such a commodity, nor is there production of a surplus which can be privately appropriated. If monopolists should allow growing consumption of this commodity in the form in which it is known today, and, in general, if they should leave up to consumers the initiative in determining its mode of production, the capitalist system would be headed toward a rapid break-up. These comments are a useful introduction to the analysis which follows.

6

THE ROLE OF CONSUMPTION IN THE CAPITALIST ECONOMY

W e have already observed that, in the long run, Engel's law —through the differentiation of profit rates—determines the prices of the different commodities and, *pro tanto*, may be considered a law of value. We have also noticed that the prevalent market form in the economy is monopolistic, and that the entrepreneurial class is capable of maintaining equilibrium in the economy according to its own complex of aims which itself also represents a law of value. Thus we face two laws of value and must consider whether, and how, they can be reconciled. For this purpose, it is necessary to examine the role of consumption in our model.

GROWTH OF CONSUMPTION

The growth of consumption is strictly linked to the development process; it must be considered a necessary, but not also a sufficient, condition of economic growth. These propositions, even though quite obvious, must be demonstrated. According to many economists, economic growth would tend to conflict, in the long run, with a saturation level of consumption. Although one segment of this school of thought seems to imply that this obstacle arises more from the impossibility of increasing consumption of individual commodities than from the impossibility of increasing total consumption, it is often implicit in the thesis of many economists that capitalist development will experience a *general* problem of consumption. In fact, it is a common postulate of a large proportion of the economic literature that, with the growth of income, the marginal utility of income will decline, and this observation is immediately applicable to consumption.[1]

---

[1] Keynes is certainly in this current of thought. Almost all growth models rest on this postulate, even though they show consumption rising *ad infinitum*. For a few clear references to the postulate, see R. F. Kahn, "The Pace of Development," in *The Challenge of Development* (Jerusalem, 1958), par. 5; R. F. Harrod, *Towards a Dynamic Economics*, pp. 36–41; and A. K. Sen, "Some Notes on the Choice of Capital Intensity in Development Planning," *Quarterly Journal of Economics* (November, 1957). Furthermore, even in the more restricted field of consumption function analyses, the different hy-

The problem is, in other words, to know whether or not there is a saturation level of global consumption. Elsewhere I have tried to establish a logical foundation for a continuously rising trend of the global value of income (of consumption).[2] It is not worthwhile here to go over that argument in detail, but it may be interesting to indicate its basis and to summarize its conclusions briefly.

THE "GENERATION" EFFECT, ENGEL'S LAW, AND NEW COMMODITIES

Let me abstract from my simplified model, for the moment, and try to consider the phenomenon of consumption in isolation. The first step is to put aside the concept of society as a sum of individuals, in order to make clear an essential characteristic. When time is taken into consideration, the structure of society changes. The individuals which compose it are not always the same and generations follow generations. These generations show a fundamental difference in relation to each other. The younger generations derive from older ones, but as a result of this background the scale of utility of the young is changed.[3] *The level of consumption reached by the older generation is a given for the following generation, and the utility which that level furnishes to the following generation is nil.* This means that the level of consumption of the

---

potheses advanced to explain the historical increase in consumption clash with the postulate of decreasing marginal utility (of income or of consumption). For example, the demonstration effect (see J. S. Duesenberry, *Income, Saving*), by which consumption increases because the lower income classes tend to emulate the higher income classes, is implicitly based on the assumption that the marginal utility of income for individual consumers does not decrease: otherwise it would be difficult to explain why there continue to exist inequalities in the "distribution" of consumption; these inequalities can be maintained only if the higher income classes also continue to increase their consumption; but these classes cannot emulate any other. This observation contains an implicit criticism of the demonstration effect: the notions of emulation drive and demonstration effect were introduced precisely to overcome the obstacle represented by the possibility that individual utilities could reach a maximum; if individual utilities did not risk reaching a maximum, there would be no need to have recourse to the demonstration effect to justify increasing consumption.

[2] "Nota sull'utilità del reddito e lo sviluppo economico," *Studi economici* (May–August, 1961).

[3] I use this language—derived from the marginalist school—only to put the question in terms which can be understood by the large majority of economists. I shall talk of social utility, although this concept cannot be measured. However, here not laws, only postulates, are being stated. Therefore, the awkwardness of the terminology does not affect the validity of the concept.

old generation is somehow an inherited part of the psychology of the individuals comprising the new generation. "Young people," in other words, do not have any idea of the experience of the generation that preceded them, and do not know that the level of consumption which they are enjoying at the initial moment of their lives has a precise location within the utility scale of each individual composing the preceding generation. They cannot conceive of a lower level of consumption than their own.

This reasoning is obviously simplified in order to permit clarity of exposition. A radical simplification, for example, is the assumption that the new generation regards as *zero* the utility it enjoys from the level of consumption reached by the preceding generation. Since generations follow each other without interruption, it would be more realistic to suppose that, for each generation, the level of consumption reached by the preceding one furnishes a (low) value of total utility. This admission does not weaken the reasoning but does complicate it. The positive value of total utility which is obtained in this way depends upon the amount of knowledge (through education, for example) that a generation has of the scale of utility of its predecessor. It is an intuitive notion, however, that the greater the time interval between generations, the less that knowledge will be. The marginal utility of consumption for each individual composing a generation does not cease to decline. However, it starts to decline from a higher initial level of utility than that of the preceding generation, and the envelope of marginal utility curves for a great number of generations slopes upward.[4] As a result, the renewal of population gives rise to an increase in the social utility of consumption, and marginal social utility does not decrease but either increases or remains constant when it is measured on the scale of utility of one of the preceding generations.

It is probably impossible to give an empirical proof of the "generation" effect. I shall consider it as another theoretical economic postulate, similar in nature to the postulate of (instantaneous) decreasing marginal utility.[5]

There exists, therefore, at least one general factor—the "genera-

---

[4] The envelope shows a tendency to increase only if each generation does not render its marginal utility zero. If this happens, the curve of marginal utility for the next generation would start from the initial level of the curve for the first generation, and the envelope would be constant. In any case, the envelope can never be decreasing.

[5] Just as this postulate is essential for static equilibrium, so our postulate is an essential condition for the rise of income in the long run.

tion" effect—which can explain the increasing trend of global consumption. This effect can also be taken as one of the possible explanations of the increase in the level of subsistence consumption. The problem of the saturation level of consumption thus shifts from the consideration of global consumption to that of the individual components of global consumption. In other words, the question becomes one of how the natural increase of consumption *manifests itself*.

In fact, there is another facet to Engel's law. Total consumption could not increase if consumption of individual commodities did not increase at different rates. The generation effect is a useful instrument in this respect and confirms Engel's law. The new generations consider as given not only the *level* of consumption reached by preceding generations (which, in any case, is an arbitrary aggregation) but also the *manifestation* of such a level in the individual commodities composing it. If it could be somehow measured, the utility of the particular ("average") combination of commodities which form the level of consumption of the preceding generation would be zero for the new generation, and a new combination of commodities is necessary to justify positive values of utility and, therefore, the desire for greater consumption.

On the other hand, Engel's law confirms the possibility of an indefinite increase in total consumption only if new commodities are continuously introduced into the economy. One would not know, otherwise, where the continuous increase in consumption as time goes on would be manifested. I do not intend to discuss in detail the role of new commodities, but I want to mention their existence as one of the assumptions which permits the working of Engel's law. Therefore, only if, together with the generation effect, new commodities are introduced from time to time in order to satisfy the continuously increasing desire for greater consumption will a saturation level of total consumption be avoided.

The elements which we have examined (the generation effect, the variation in the composition of consumption with the rise in income, the introduction of new commodities) are not unique to the capitalist economy, but are aspects of the phenomenon of consumption which are common to all economic systems. Instead, what is peculiar to the capitalist economy is the relationship between the spheres of production and of consumption, and it is necessary to examine this problem before facing the question of the role of Engel's law in our model.

PREDOMINANCE OF PRODUCTION
OVER CONSUMPTION

The concept of the market as the meeting point of consumers and producers, both independent and "sovereign" parties with different inclinations and tastes, had already been undermined in the discussion of monopolistic forms which has taken place since the work of Sraffa. Nevertheless, quite a few authors have been unable to abandon some of the concepts criticized, in particular, that of consumer sovereignty. One still can hear of a "theory of demand" and of schedules of "demand prices," based on subjective notions of utility taken as factors in the formation of prices. Yet, as has been implied in the modern discussion of the problem of value[6] and anticipated with extraordinary foresight by the classical economists, in particular by Marx, when consumption is seen dynamically, it is far from being an independent factor in the capitalist system.

Of course, the marginalists did not propose that consumption would determine production. They were only proposing that the market price would reflect, as far as possible, and at each moment of time, the inclinations of both parties in the exchange, so that neither would dominate the other. In order for this to happen, it is necessary that judgments and actions of consumers and producers be equally powerful. Not only must producers and consumers, taken individually, be powerless to dictate the price of a commodity, but they should not even have the power to dictate which commodities should be produced or consumed and in which quanti-

---

[6] The modern theory of demand subscribes only halfheartedly to the concept of consumer sovereignty: it limits itself to the analysis of consumer preferences on the market, namely, in the presence of a given price structure for available commodities. It is impossible to quote from the now vast body of literature on the subject. However, H. Uzawa ("Preference and Rational Choice in the Theory of Consumption," in K. J. Arrow et al. [eds.], *Mathematical Methods in the Social Sciences, 1959 Proceedings* [Stanford Symposium on Mathematical Methods in the Social Sciences; Stanford, Calif., 1959]) gives a clear illustration of the different theories. The critique of the subjective theory of value (in its most refined form, based on the comparison of utilities, rather than on their measurement) is included in P. Samuelson, *Foundations*, pp. 90–91. If utility cannot be measured, comparisons among utilities and analysis of consumer preferences can only be undertaken by ascertaining the actual choices made by consumers on the market—choices which are already weighted by the existing prices. Therefore, consumer behavior cannot be derived from the complex of preferences. As a result, even in the marginalist scheme, demand does not seem to have a sovereign nature.

ties (in other words, they should not be able to dictate the structure of values and of prices of commodities).

However, the inclinations and tastes of consumers in fact depend on production, when they are viewed in a dynamic setting, because they can only be manifested *when commodities are already present on the market.* If certain commodities are not available on the market, the consumer will not be able to make a choice among them (the utility of a non-existing commodity is an absurd concept). Production, therefore, by the mere act of making a commodity available, determines its consumption. If the type and the number of commodities present on the market are determined by production, the choices of consumers are no longer the result of a subjective and sovereign judgment: the freedom of the consumer is already somehow limited by the particular variety of commodities which are being offered. The fundamental behavioral laws of the consumer—like Engel's law—would therefore acquire validity only *after* the availability of certain commodities has been established in the market. This is not enough. Since commodities are already in the market, they must already have a price, since they certainly had a production cost. But if the different commodities have a price, the consumers' judgment regarding their (relative) utility will be somehow influenced by those prices (the "primitive" structure of prices). The value scale of the economic system, therefore, has been formed, in essence, even before the consumer—in his role as an entity separate from the producer— comes upon the scene. Historically, this is obvious: the capitalist system emerges from an older social order where relative values have been already established. The "new" aspect of the capitalist system is not the existence of consumers, but the existence of capitalistic producers. Thus, the new mode of social production generates new values and new prices. This form of predominance of production becomes more evident when one considers the well-known fact that, at any given moment and in a market, individual consumers are unable to determine their "independent" preference, since they find themselves confronting a well-established price system. It is also true, on the other hand, that this form of production predominance does not imply that consumers are obliged to consume what they do not want. In other words, consumer tastes have some weight in the determination of production, even though they are neither independent nor sovereign.

The analysis, however, cannot stop at this stage. The Marxian school, for example, after having pointed out its subjugation to production, has not continued to examine the tendencies and the effects of consumption. Even in these pages, the structure of prices has been considered to be determined exclusively by Engel's law. It is now the moment to face the question of the reconciliation of Engel's law with the predominance of production.

PRODUCTION PREDOMINANCE AND ENGEL'S LAW

If the availability of commodities on the market and the "primitive" price structure can influence consumer choices, the consumer tendency to diversify consumption certainly cannot be ignored. On the other hand, although both the postulate of the indefinite increase of consumption (the generation effect) and Engel's law represent fundamental psychological laws, which are operative in all economic systems, they are not capable of explaining why certain tendencies rather than others are present in the evolution of the consumer budget in a capitalist society. What Engel's law does not say is as important, if not more important, than what it does say.

Let us suppose that the subsistence level of consumption is easily identifiable.[7] Beyond this level, the classification of needs as primary or secondary does not have the force of necessity. As a first approximation, it could be said that the gradation of needs depends on the social milieu—with its complex of traditional customs—in which individuals live,[8] but it could also be said that the social milieu depends on the preferences, and thus on the grading of needs, of individuals. By considering individuals outside their social milieu, it is possible to say, for example, that a higher level of education can be considered more important than the ownership of an automobile or of a house of a particular type; but it is also possible to say the contrary. What does determine the particular scale of priority in goods consumed at the different stages of development of the capitalist society—in relation to other social systems, present and past—is a fundamental interpretive problem of a distinctive character, which is among the most important issues of capitalism.

In substance, two questions remain open after the introduction

---

[7] In the real world, consumers can make a choice even within this level, since it is possible to mix the elements of a minimum biological diet in different ways; we have not taken this case into account.

[8] This is the thesis of T. Veblen, "The Limitation of Marginal Utility," in *The Place of Science in Modern Civilization and Other Essays* (New York, 1932).

of Engel's law: (1) why just that particular consumer budget with just those tendencies can be observed in the capitalist system; and (2) who or what determines the new consumer budgets arising from Engel's law, and for what purposes and for what reasons. These questions, of course, are part of only one reality, and by analyzing them one aims at discovering the *true* rationalizing principle of the economic process. Whether one follows this path—and examines the character of consumption—or follows the classical Ricardian-Marxian path, which starts from the examination of the structure of production, should make no fundamental difference, since the predominance of production over consumption makes the later a reflection of the former.

Although history has for its subject matter different civilizations which are differentiated, *inter alia*, by the form in which the social surplus is consumed, capitalism—although it shows a new form of surplus consumption—is different from previous social forms because *the aim of the system does not lie in the consumption of a particular commodity*. If the modern economic history of Continental European countries and of England is examined, even superficially, it can easily be seen that the consumer budget does not show a tendency toward this or that particular commodity which would represent the aim of the whole social structure. There exists, however, a body of opinion which would identify capitalism with a particular form of consumption (the means of transportation, for example) and concludes therefrom that capitalism is destined to disappear as soon as that type of consumption clashes with the necessary variability of consumer budgets, as dictated by Engel's law.[9] It would seem that history, which demonstrates the variability of consumption in capitalist societies, has disposed of this opinion.

The aim of capitalism is not a particular form of social consumption, then, but a particular form of productive structure, whose means of attainment is dependent upon a variety of forms of social consumption. It is true, of course, that not all forms of consumption, and therefore not all forms of production, are always compatible with the capitalist structure of production. The way in which Engel's law is determined in capitalism—always underlining the fact that Engel's law is present in all expanding economic systems—indicates clearly, it seems to me, that the rationalizing prin-

[9] This current of thought is linked with the liberal-radical school.

ciple of the system resides in the entrepreneurs. As we have already observed, one has to leave behind the illusion of the existence of an interplay of demand and supply among equally independent and sovereign subjects which would determine the structure of production as a function of the tastes and the choices of consumers (in harmony with the possible development of productive processes).[10] Since the capitalist system has succeeded in completely isolating the functions of the producer from those of the consumer through the creation of a market, and since the consumer can make his choices only within the framework of the commodities available on the market, entrepreneurs are capable—within the limits of Engel's law—of determining the form of consumption that will be most convenient for them.

I shall try to illustrate this proposition. Although a solution is not obtainable, I shall at least attempt to provide indications of where it might lie. The way in which entrepreneurs give content to Engel's law is so simple that it may seem a tautology. We should not picture for ourselves the entrepreneurial class as a "board of governors" which makes decisions valid for the system as a whole. What entrepreneurs do not want is that consumption should grow in such a way as to require increasing quantities of commodities that are not "suitable" to the capitalist system. An "unsuitable" commodity is here defined as a commodity which vitiates the fundamental principle of the system: the private appropriation of means of production.[11] Now, entrepreneurs are already acting through a capitalist system of production *and cannot fall into a contradiction by producing "unsuitable" commodities*: the new commodities that they will introduce on the market will always be satisfactory, for the purposes of Engel's law, and will not endanger the capitalist structure of production. On the other hand, consumers are not stupid: each new commodity introduced on the

[10] Even setting aside what was said in the preceding paragraph, the existence of monopolies as a necessary element in the working of the system implies a subordinate position of consumers.

[11] In dealing with a commodity which is not suitable to capitalist production, the possibility is not excluded that another compatible commodity can be introduced to satisfy the same need. Although this observation reduces the argument to a tautology, it is still useful in order to ascertain that production determines consumption: a particular structure of consumption will not be permitted by the system unless it can be expressed in commodities which are compatible with the capitalist structure of production. It is not easy, however, to cite examples of commodities which are unsuitable, for reasons which will be seen more clearly below. Perhaps it is not even appropriate here.

market must satisfy a need, and it is not certain that any commodity will, *ipso facto*, satisfy Engel's law. Each new commodity introduced by entrepreneurs will go to increase the number of commodities present on the market: it will then be the consumers who will determine which among these will in fact satisfy Engel's law.

While the possibility that individual commodities that might compromise the stability of the system may be supplied on the market is in this way excluded, it is logically necessary to exclude also the possibility that the whole batch of consumed commodities may become "unsuitable" in relation to the capitalist system of production. One can conceive of a total consumption which, although composed of commodities which are individually suitable, presents a composition of different types of commodities which is not suitable. It is difficult to give examples. Just to illustrate the point, one can imagine as unsuitable a composition of consumption in which professional services, although ordinarily suitable commodities, exceed a certain percentage of total expenditure. The argument which was presented above relating to individual commodities is applicable in this case as well. Since producers act within a certain framework of weights, and therefore of values, given to the different needs and to the commodities which satisfy them, entrepreneurs cannot fall into a contradiction by permitting a framework of weights and values which is not harmonious with the system in which they are operating.[12] It seems also reasonable to suppose that the capitalist system of priorities (the complex of aims) derives, at least in part, from the "primitive" structure of prices that appears when the functions of the producer and of the consumer are completely separated—when the private appropriation of means of production occurs. The two factors which we have seen to limit the choice of consumers appear again on the scene: the mere availability of certain commodities on the market, which prevents the choice of unsuitable commodities; and the "primitive" structure of prices, which prevents the choice of a whole batch of unsuitable consumed commodities.

In proposing the predominance of production over consumption and the ability of entrepreneurs to give meaning to Engel's law, the

---

[12] By saying that entrepreneurs cannot permit an unsuitable composition of consumption, I mean that the class is composed of members for whom the characteristics of capitalist production are so much taken for granted that they cannot conceive of a different system. This observation also, of course, becomes tautological in the moment of application.

intention is only to show that it is *the capitalist system itself* that gives meaning to Engel's law, so as to assure its own continuity and its own predominance. The implication is not that individual entrepreneurs can determine the consumption of the commodities produced by them. It is possible for the consumer to choose among different commodities in the capitalist system, though within the limits indicated above; there exists an appearance of freedom without which the system would, in fact, become unbearable. Within these limits, the development of consumption will cause a change in the structure of prices and in the structure of profit rates.

From the point of view of economic doctrine, the situation depicted has peculiar characteristics. In brief, both consumption and production have a role in the economic development of capitalism, but it is capitalist production, and not consumption, that determines the whole complex of social-economic relationships, which in the final analysis, constitute the essence of the system.

THE MARKET

Although in our model there is no place for a freely competitive market, the concept of "market" does not lose its significance. It is precisely from the freedom (even though limited) of the consumer, stemming from Engel's law and from the presence of a market in which this law can express itself, that the phenomenon of profit rate differentiation derives. Since the dynamics of prices depends on Engel's law, as the expression of the psychology of consumers, and since this dynamics is applied to a complex of commodities, as the expression of the aims of entrepreneurs, the market is the natural meeting place of these tendencies. Given the correspondence of the development of each enterprise with the over-all aims of the entrepreneurial class, the market thus allows entrepreneurs to control the price structure, within Engel's law, without recourse to more formal organs of direction. The market represents the means by which the capitalist system succeeds in isolating the functions of consumers from those of producers, so that the fundamental behavioral laws of consumption can find a correspondence in the system of aims (and thus of values) of entrepreneurs.

CONTROLS OF THE ENTREPRENEURIAL CLASS

Even though it would seem "unnatural" for the capitalist system to create within itself commodities which could endanger its equilibrium, it does not follow that equilibrium will be maintained at all times. On the one hand, to give even an "appearance" of freedom to consumers in their choices may be sufficient to let loose a chain reaction if consumers become conscious of their subordinate position. On the other hand, entrepreneurs themselves as individuals can misinterpret the aims of the class and allow production of unsuitable commodities; although they cannot, of necessity, make this type of mistake for the products of their own enterprise, they can make mistakes when the effects of their production on the production of other enterprises are considered (the production of a commodity—even a suitable commodity—may require means of production, or may lead to the consumption of complementary commodities, which are not suitable). Similarly, although according to our reasoning entrepreneurs cannot act in a contradictory manner by permitting a schedule of consumed commodities which is unsuitable to capitalist production, there always exists a risk that a single entrepreneur may make mistakes or may not recognize the scale of values of a system (this is all the more relevant when the market form is monopolistic).

I have explained in a general way how entrepreneurs become the rationalizing principle of the capitalist economy. With the same degree of generality I shall indicate the means by which entrepreneurs succeed in directing production and in controlling consumption. The class uses social-political means, some with an over-all influence on the economy (wars, revolutions, etc.), others with a more limited influence (government intervention, the recognition of trade unions, etc.), with which it controls the social form of the system in relation to both production and consumption, and the rate of capital accumulation, respectively; through the economic policies of governments (for example, anticyclical policies, the regulation of monopolies), the class reserves for itself principally the control of short-term movements and also, in part, the direct control of production and consumption (for example, monetary and fiscal policies). The structure and development of consumption and of production are also influenced by a series of other social-economic factors: in addition to the demonstration effect, already discussed (see p. 119, n. 1), larger social-cultural myths and, consequently, rules of law and of praxis are created. The educational system, of course, represents the most direct means of influencing the batch of consumed commodities.[13] It is precisely because of the comprehensiveness of class influence that historians call capitalist society a civilization.

CONCLUSION

While Engel's law identifies the mode of development of consumption and *pro tanto* determines the structure of prices and changes in that structure, the aims of the entrepreneurial class determine the content of Engel's law and, consequently, determine the structure and development of prices in the first place. The change in the technical conditions of production does not influence the price system or its orderly development if it is neutral, and this change is always neutral, in a closed economy,[14] with the exception of an efficiency law of technical progress by which the most dynamic enterprises are favored and the natural development of relative prices is facilitated. Thus, the growth of the capitalist system, permitted by the continuous introduction of technical progress, depends on the development of consumption as dictated by Engel's law, in ways not inconsistent with the goals of the entrepreneurial class, which, recognizing itself as such by means of a monopolistic market structure again created in its turn by Engel's law, maintains the economic system in equilibrium in the long run.

[13] I am aware that these forms of control are logically weak, primarily because it is difficult to ascertain the precise relationship between the influence of social-economic habits and a "correct" behavior of entrepreneurs. This is another theme which deserves further study.

[14] And for all capitalist economies.

CONCLUDING NOTES

I. PRICES AND VALUES

After having examined the structure and growth of the capitalist system in some of its essential aspects, it is necessary to reconsider the problem of measurement. We have already seen that this problem is rapidly becoming an obstacle to the development of modern economic theory, much in the same way as it has inscribed classical and neoclassical analyses in a vicious circle. It is not, of course, only the question of measuring capital which represents an obstacle, but the larger question of measuring values.

In the description undertaken above, Engel's law plays an important role in the determination of economic growth. In the long run, it determines the continuous variation in the composition of consumption and, consequently, in the composition of production. Considering the economy as a whole, the change in the structure of production causes a change in the relative prices of commodities, as time goes on and income increases: this variation is continuous and essential for economic growth. When relative prices change, however, it is not possible to use index numbers to compare prices of individual commodities and, therefore, to measure the value of total income, of investment, of consumption, and of all other economic aggregates. This difficulty, which faces the external observer, also affects economic agents. In fact, not even individual enterprises are capable of providing satisfactory objective measures for comparing balance sheets at different moments of time,[1] even if their ability to make decisions is not necessarily

[1] A Dutch firm has attempted to build its financial statements by evaluating the different items at constant prices, primarily in order to eliminate the influence of inflation. Apart from the fact that in this way inflation caused by exceptional circumstances is not distinguished from inflation caused by pressures inherent in the economic structure of a country, the procedure itself (see A. Goudeket, "An Application of Replacement Value Theory," *Journal of Accountancy* [July, 1960]) is based on the deflation of items of a general nature (profits, reserves, etc.) by means of a general price index. Such a procedure is, however, self-defeating. It cannot be used by all the enterprises in one economy without becoming a vicious circle: because the price index is based on a certain proportion of different components, and because this proportion changes over time, the index becomes useless as time goes on, but if

affected. This is the reason why, in describing the system, a note of pessimism was injected about the possibility of discovering a relationship between prices and values which could be anticipated by an external interpreter. It seems worth while to examine this question more closely.

According to our argument, prices of different commodities, given the validity of Engel's law and the ability of the capitalist system always to produce a rate of accumulation which is compatible with the maintenance of equilibrium, will be such as to assure a greater rate of profits, in the long run, for the commodities produced by the industries that satisfy a consumption growing at a faster rate than consumption of commodities produced by other industries. In other words, commodities will exchange among themselves at a rate of exchange (price) such that some commodities will show a rate of profit on the means of production sufficient to permit a more rapid increase in productive capacity and in output than other commodities. Since changes in techniques are neutral or, if not neutral, follow this law, changes in relative values (prices) of commodities will therefore have a strict relationship to the change in the underlying physical quantities. This rule, however, is far from being a law of value. To say that commodities are traded as a function of the rate of growth of relative consumption means that prices refer only to commodities which are present on the market at any moment of time. But since the commodity mix present on the market changes in the long run—new commodities are introduced and constitute the basis for the change in subsistence consumption—the exchange relationship indicated above can be distinguished only moment by moment and only for existing commodities: it is not valid, therefore, in the long run, or in other words, its limited validity does not provide a general law of value. Although actual prices obviously indicate moment by moment a measure of value, the system also grows through the introduction of new commodities, and these alter the system of relative prices in a completely unforeseeable fashion. The relationship between prices and the development of consumption will thus be an expression of the law of value only *ex post facto*.

---

all enterprises were to adopt it, the index could change the tendency of the economy and oblige enterprises to respect its original composition. In general, since inflation is certainly linked to the change in the structure of the index, to eliminate the effect of inflation in this way is clearly wrong.

Prices, as we have seen, are both a reflection of the laws of the development of consumption and an indication of the aims of the system: as such, they are also a measure of efficiency. The dynamics of price originates, in the long run, from Engel's law and from the "appearance" of freedom given to consumers in the choice of commodities which satisfy Engel's law, since the choice of consumers is exercised on commodities which are always compatible with the complex of aims of the entrepreneurial class; logically, therefore, the aims of the class will have been established *before* prices, and thus prices will be the faithful image of the aims, the means by which the complex of values of the entrepreneurial class is realized.[2]

We meet here another apparent contradiction. How can the entrepreneurial class, formed of monopolists who know only more or less approximately the effects of their decisions on the economy as a whole, satisfy its aims without being able to evaluate the results of its actions in the long run, since it does not possess a true measure? As has already been indicated, the hypothesis of "omniscience" of the entrepreneurial class rests on the capacity of the class to become self-aware as soon as an event (endogenous or exogenous) which may change the orderly growth of the system occurs. In the long run, the class is always capable of remedying possible disequilibria. Even if it cannot calculate in terms of a true measure the position of an economy at a certain moment in relation to a previous moment or to a later moment, the entrepreneurial class will be aware that an undesired change has happened, say, in the "average" profit rate or in the share of profits in total income. Since this limited awareness is sufficient to allow the system to continue indefinitely, there is no reason to think that there exists a real contradiction between the predominance of the class and its inability to evaluate different situations by an unchanging yardstick. What has been postulated as a measure of output—the existence of an historical-social value judgment—is nothing more than the capacity of the class, as the subject of the economic system, to make rational choices. Thus, *the measure of value lies within the entrepreneurial class itself*, and is determined by the class's own

[2] While in the long run the relationship between the predominance of supply and Engel's law can be reasonably interpreted, in the short run the mechanism through which that relationship is expressed is too confused and complex to be subjected to analysis. Similarly confused is the process by which the aims of the class are specified in day-to-day activities.

aims and by the order that the capitalist system creates in civil society. The time continuity which would be assured by an unchanging measure of value is instead assured by the continuity of the class itself. In conclusion, if consumption, prices, and the relationships among values are all determined by the entrepreneurs, the system does not need a measure of value which would be valid in the long run.

The independent observer is thus incapable in the long run of evaluating with precision the same position at two different moments of time. But does not such inability represent a philosophical impossibility? When the composition of consumption changes, and when the relationships among sectors change, can one say (once the biological level of subsistence has been left behind) that a "better" position has been reached? Would not such a "better" position represent a value judgment expressed not by the independent observer, but by the subjects of the economic process? And would not such a value judgment be identical to that which welfare theory has in vain tried to assess during half a century of discussions on the concept of the optimum? If it is the subjects of the economic process who themselves establish what is "better" in relation to their own goals, is it not that complex of goals itself the yardstick by which one should evaluate each economic system? And since this yardstick is the expression of a complex of goals of a particular class of individuals, how could it ever be applied by external observers[3] so as to make it an exact measure?

Although these are leading questions, they do not give support to a position of scientific nihilism, tending to annul the functions of the interpreter. On the contrary, a judgment or comparison between two economies in the long run is a judgment of a political-social nature from which the economist is excluded only if he stays within the context of neoclassical methodology and formulation. But there is nothing which prevents an economist from tackling larger interpretive problems by using a dialectic method. Moreover, when the economist operates within any one complex of goals and in the shortest period, he is perfectly able to conduct analyses even without recourse to dialectics. However, for long-period analyses, economists will never find a true measure of value; any attempt to

---

[3] It seems difficult to believe that it would be applied by observers who are members of the class, since the fact of their participation in it would make them incapable of seeing objectively the phenomena surrounding them.

do so by means of restrictive hypotheses is bound to distort the character of the system under study.

I have tried to demonstrate that, even in the absence of a true measure of value that would permit a precise comparison of different economic systems and a judgment on their "optimality," there exist rational subjects of the economic process. In the capitalist system, entrepreneurs, conscious of themselves as a class, *naturally* impose on the society a complex of aims by which, in the long run, the entrepreneurial class itself evaluates the efficiency of the tools which it has adopted and the orders it has given to the system. The self-awareness of the class must not be understood as the creation of permanent formal organs of direction, but rather as an occasional intervention each time the system appears to be breaking down either as a result of the pressure of external forces or as a result of possible internal contradictions. In any case, if a formal organ of direction is lacking, the class does possess, I think, what can on occasion become a powerful tool at its service: the state.

II. DYNAMICS AND DIALECTICS

The model that has been presented is a dynamic, not a dialectic one. The distinction is important, beyond all the ideological characterizations that the term "dialectics" may have acquired. Since Marx, very little dialectics has penetrated economic science. On the one hand, Marxist authors (with the exceptions of Luxemburg and Hilferding) were largely satisfied with Marx's original analysis from the dialectic point of view. Also, once an example of a non-capitalist system was established, it was difficult to deal with the dialectic substance of that system without bringing it into the discussion (fortunately, this attitude is now changing). On the other hand, non-Marxist authors cannot fully digest a dialectic vision of economics for two reasons: (1) their inbred incapacity to pass from empiricism to more general types of logic; and (2) their implicit recognition, in admitting a dialectic procedure, that the model analyzed by them, far from being an abstract representation of any kind of economic system, is in fact to a large extent a picture of a particular historical system. For whatever reason, a dialectic discussion of economics has not appeared since the classics. My own resources are too meager to undertake this step, and I will limit myself to only a few observations.

The reader may have noticed that I have not discussed the possible antithesis of each of the theses advanced in my model. Even the contradictions of the capitalist system that have been pointed out —e.g., the need to control the profit motive to permit the rise in wages, the lack of equilibrium in an open economy, etc.—are little more than incidents in the exposition, and may well be a result of insufficient knowledge on my part or of some peculiarity of the model itself. To start with, there exist two ways of being dynamic in economics. A first, rudimentary, way is to add time as a dimension to known variables, and then to find out what happens to them.[4] A dynamics of this kind is really little more than statics,

---

[4] This is roughly the procedure adopted by M. Kalecki, in his *Economic Dynamics*.

since no new variable or new relationship between variables is established by such a procedure. A second, less rudimentary, way is to study the dynamic behavior of the system as a whole and to isolate those variables or relationships which arise only when time is introduced. This is the procedure adopted by many modern economists (including Mrs. Robinson, who is possibly the best example), and by practically all the classical authors.[5] This second method has been followed in my model.

But a dynamic treatment is a weak tool if, instead of descriptions, one is interested in interpretations. Dynamics, by definition, studies a model in equilibrium. Although it investigates the forces which may or may not make this equilibrium stable, its terms of reference remain those of an equilibrium system in which all contradictions are solved. The weakness of the approach is evident. If the model is in equilibrium, the economist is not really trying to interpret the reality of this or that system, but only of the model itself. In these models, the structure of a system is typified and *immobilized*; there will continue to be x number of classes, y number of sectors, z number of equations. This is, of course, not a defect of the models, but of the approach. Also it is not a defect at all if economics is intended to be confined to the shortest possible time period. The dynamic approach is not improved if, instead of applying it to an equilibrium model, one focuses attention on a disequilibrium model. The latter, as is well known, is nothing but the former with different parameter values and does not do away with the problem of the immobility of dynamics.

A qualitative jump is necessary. In addition to statics and dynamics, economists cannot avoid studying the logic of the possible contradictions included in the *structure* of the economic system under consideration. The questions to be answered are: what are the invisible but real forces which can arise from an equilibrium behavior of a system's variables? Which structural aspect of the economy is liable to lead to a contradiction in the life of the system?

The number of possibilities open to analysis is enormous. Any aspect of capitalism—whether or not peculiar to that system—can justify a full-fledged study of a dialectic character. In the following pages I have tried to list only some of the more promising ones.

The first, and possibly the most serious, contradiction in the

---

[5] For an analysis of the two types of dynamics, see J. R. Hicks, *Growth and Capital* (Oxford, 1965).

capitalist system may lie in the profit motive. As we have seen, if the profit motive of individual entrepreneurs is left unchecked, it can rapidly destroy the economy by drying up demand, either through a reduction or through an insufficient increase in wages and their consequences for sales and profits themselves. This contradiction can be resolved by introducing the notion of an entrepreneurial class. However, in a system of differentiated profit rates, a balance between this feature and the profit motive can only be struck if entrepreneurs are subdivided on the basis of profit classes. The possible contradiction arising from having an entrepreneurial class subdivided into classes was solved in my model by making the entrepreneurial class dependent on monopolistic conditions on the market. The non-monopolists, therefore, do not participate in the regulating functions of the class.

This picture has all the features of an exploding structure. No matter how strongly entrenched is each class, the profit motive is present, and its peculiarity is that it acts as a maximizing agent at all times. Therefore, entrepreneurs who are condemned to a lower rate of profit will always try to overtake those who are privileged with a higher one. If this happens, the growth of the economy is endangered because it will show an equiproportionate sectoral trend incompatible with Engel's law. But if this does not happen, the profit motive itself, given enough time, will disappear.

A possible solution to this contradiction is a stronger tendency toward mergers, the smaller entrepreneurs becoming participants with the bigger ones in the latter's higher profits. Aside from the fact that in so doing small entrepreneurs will lose their personality and therefore may not collaborate in the process, a general tendency toward mergers would make the capitalist system vulnerable to yet a different set of contradictions, arising from the possible differences between consumer desires and available supply. The dominance of the latter over the former can exist and continue while it remains within "reasonable" confines. When it surpasses these confines (in arms production, for example), it endangers itself.

The economics of mergers is also interesting for another reason. The balance, in big enterprises, between centralization and decentralization is an evident manifestation of dialectics in the capitalist system. The dilemma is well known and is encountered in all types of economies: the greater efficiency of decentralization tends to dismember centralized entities. The system of relative prices, to change which is within the power of the supply side, can be influenced to their advantage by decentralized units of big enterprises almost as much as it is influenced by individual enterprises. The consequences for the capitalist system are not clear, but their importance cannot be discounted.

Another possible contradiction arises from the regulating function which the entrepreneurial class allocates to itself, and the decline of the workers as a class. The more technical progress injected into the capitalist economy and the more leisure time gained by the workers, the less is the scope of trade unions. The numerical decline of the working class—as distinct from blue-collar workers —is a well-documented fact. Although the phenomenon has been studied by sociologists, its economic significance has not been appreciated.

The fewer workers there are, the weaker the class ties among workers are, and the weaker their bargaining power in terms of wages is. The non-entrepreneurs become a subsidized group whose main function is that of consuming commodities sold by entrepreneurs. A contradiction emerges. The entrepreneurial class will have to intervene more often in order to permit wages to rise. If, in so doing, it must establish itself as a permanent "directorate," the system will fall into a trap: *as soon as the class is formally organized, the profit motive ceases to exist.*

As this process unfolds, wages do rise. It is reasonable to assume that workers or non-entrepreneurs will acquire ownership of the means of production controlled by the entrepreneurial class. This is not, however, a salvaging feature. If non-entrepreneurs cannot form themselves into a class, their acquisition of property will be just another form of diluted capitalism, and entrepreneurs will not be affected. Even if they do form a class and exercise control over their whole share of property, they will still delegate its management to entrepreneurs. No real dialectics of interests is created, and the profit motive is still endangered.

Is the capitalist system a set of mechanisms geared to ration scarce commodities, and, in this case, could it withstand abundance? This question is related to that of ownership and the price (cost) of ownership. If a system develops its set of aims and of values by establishing prices, it is likely that it will not be able to adapt to a *zero price system.* If ownership is maintained beyond the stage at which the commodity owned has become a free commodity, the system will be inherently unable to withstand abundance. It is not easy to picture the way in which the obvious contradiction could manifest itself.

It is possible that the setting up of a value relationship where value is non-existent might produce a tendency towards excessive accumulation, which no class directorate could remedy. Consumption would always tend to be insufficient. Also, the differentiation of profit rates could be in contrast with Engel's law, since certain economic activities would receive a remuneration out of keeping with their development needs. In any case, a system which is based on ownership as a mechanism for income distribution, for credit activities, and for tax purposes can hardly be considered efficient when the value of ownership progressively nears zero.

These are only a few examples, but if economists consider them to be relevant, the area to be investigated is great indeed. This line of attack may well lead to new forms of ideology rather than to the refinement of our understanding of social changes. The risk is, in my opinion, worth taking. In its investigative moments science is always ideology.

APPENDIX A

PROBLEMS OF AN OPEN ECONOMY

I n the principal text I limited my observations to the case of a closed economy. Let us now enlarge the field of analysis and observe the structure of the capitalist system in the context of an economy open to trade with other economies. I shall not undertake a detailed analysis of the generalized model but limit myself to observing how some of the new elements that have been introduced in the text are modified.

In defining an open economy we will admit that there exist a number of economies with different characteristics which influence each other. For example, among the restrictive assumptions on which our closed model was based was that of an homogeneous distribution of natural resources. When an open economy is considered, variations in natural resources among different economies become relevant. Other peculiarities—social, historical, climatic, etc.—are also responsible for differences in the structures of open economies. Since I cannot examine all the possible differences among open economies, the following analysis will be concentrated on two particularly important problems: the first is the change in the technical conditions of production; the second, the international consequences of a differentiated structure of profit rates. In both cases, some light will be shed on a few more obscure relationships. The second problem, however, is particularly difficult. (In considering the relationships among different economies, it will be assumed that ours remains a capitalist universe.)

TECHNICAL CONDITIONS OF PRODUCTION

In an isolated economy, technical conditions of production change as a function of technical progress. There is no reason to suppose that entrepreneurs will choose among different techniques having different degrees of mechanization according to the changes in the rates of profits and of wages: each new technique requires an equal innovative effort, from a technological point of view, quite apart from the productivity which characterizes it. These propositions were illustrated (see p. 76) by having recourse to the observation that, at the logical initial moment of the process of economic growth, there exists only one technique. Wherever the process of growth has taken place, in that place the first superior technique was created. From that moment on, the different techniques in each production line succeed each other in a superiority relationship.

In observing an open economy, the possibility arises that a superior technique developed in one economy will not be superior when it is applied to another economy in which the mix of natural resources is different. If a technique which is superior for one economy is not superior for another, considering the two economies as one system, at the same moment of time we will be able to observe a number of techniques which are not superior to each other. This situation, in time, will allow a choice, of the neoclassical type, among techniques having different degrees of mechanization, according to the relative changes in profit and wage rates. However, it is possible to show that technical progress expands from one economy to the other, irrespective of the supply of natural resources, in such a way that production techniques do not lose their continuous relationship of superiority.

We must start by examining, one by one, the production techniques which are present in one economy, leaving aside, for the moment, the concept of a technique as a complex of productive processes forming the production structure of an economy. Let us suppose that the composition of output does not change. Alternatively, we may suppose that we can express quantitatively the historical-social judgment by which a change in the composition of output can be translated into an increase in output. Let us choose one technique, a method of production which is unique in the production line of the economy under consideration, and which is superior to any other previously existing methods of production.

Whatever the deep economic and historical reasons that have caused this technique to become available in an economy having a given mix of natural resources, it, necessarily, is also superior for all the other economies which form our economic universe. At the (logical) initial moment of the growth process, the first superior techniques have been invented and applied in one particular location. No technique, prior to that moment, was superior to another one, nor did there exist a variety of techniques. If a variety of techniques existed, even though they were distributed among different economies, it would be necessary to assume a prior inventive activity. But such activity, if it had been applied to only one technique, would have created superior techniques, not a variety of alternative techniques, since they are equally difficult to invent. If in that moment there were a variety of non-superior techniques, we would not be at the initial moment of the growth process. For as long as the possibility of an inventive activity applied to the economy can be admitted, one must go back in time. It is only when one assumes *a single* initial technique for different economies that it is possible to define the initial moment of the growth process. The "primeval" technique must therefore be identical in all economies at the initial moment of the growth process. As soon as an economy develops a superior method of production, it will be introduced in all other economies, and for them as well that method will be superior.[1]

In conclusion, whatever the mix of natural resources which characterizes each economy, the most recent technique in one economy will be superior for all other economies, including those that begin their development process late. Following this argument, less advanced countries, in planning their development, should always choose the latest technique elaborated by more advanced countries because it will certainly be superior.[2]

An example may clarify the argument. To produce commodity *a* there exists a production technique developed much earlier. Following the argument which links the logical origin of the development process to the existence of only one primitive technique for each production line in all economies, the technique producing commodity *a* will be common to all economies. Let us suppose that

---

[1] Given the distance between economies and the differences in economic and social environments, some countries may well continue to use techniques which are obsolete in another country; however, what is important is that superior techniques are available if countries want to change technology.

[2] This result differs from current opinion. It is often said that an underdeveloped country, in order to optimize its growth path, should follow all the steps of the economic process already experienced in now advanced economies, and therefore it should adopt techniques which are less "advanced" than the techniques used at present in the industrialized countries. R. Nurkse (*Problems of Capital Formation in Underdeveloped Countries* [Oxford, 1953]) maintains that backward economies with surplus labor do not need tools and machines which have the same degree of capital intensity as those used in advanced economies, where labor is relatively scarce. M. H. Dobb (*Economic Growth and Underdeveloped Countries* [London, 1963]) criticizes this opinion, which is rapidly becoming accepted because of its formal plausibility, although it is certainly wrong since, *inter alia*, it does not distinguish between technical progress and changes in capital intensity.

in economy X, where there exists abundant manpower (in comparison with economy Y), a new superior technique to produce commodity *a* is now developed. It may well be that such a technique[3] utilizes labor inputs to a greater extent than a superior technique in the same production line would have if developed in economy Y. However, the technique developed by X will also be superior for Y. At the level of each technique, therefore, the difference in natural resources (social, historical, educational, etc.) is not significant.

This difference, on the other hand, is significant when one considers the economy as a whole. Let us suppose that the new superior techniques are always and exclusively created in economy X and only later introduced into economy Y. These techniques, taken one by one, reflect in some way the natural resource mix of X. Since this mix is different from that of Y, the effects of the new technique coming from X, although always superior, may have a neutral or biased character. A technique which is superior and neutral in one country remains superior but may become capital-using or capital-saving in the other economy, depending on the rates of profits and wages prevalent there. Thus the international dissemination of what was originally neutral technical progress may result in biased technical progress for individual economies in terms of their resource mix.

Although in the short period these differences may produce non-neutral tendencies in each economy, in the long period they need not have the same effect. If there exists a great number of different economies, each one producing new techniques, and if there exists an extensive exchange of technical know-how among economies, it is reasonable to suppose that, for each economy, the character of the different superior techniques will distribute itself *at random* among the neutral, the capital-using and the capital-saving characters. The character of technical progress in this case will be a random variable which can take only three values with constant probability, the average value of which corresponds to the neutral character.[4]

The law of neutrality is not valid, however, when technical progress originates almost exclusively in economies that show a long-run profit-wage relationship different from that prevailing in the

---

[3] For this type of question, see Appendix B.

[4] A similar argument has been used in the context of a closed economy; see Chapter 4, above, pp. 82–83.

economies that receive the innovations. In the real world, innovations are created principally in the industrialized countries (e.g., the United States, the United Kingdom), where the relationship between wage and profit rates is different from that of underdeveloped countries. In this case, a neutral innovation in the former will most probably be capital-using in the latter.

This asymmetry raises another problem regarding the effects of the international dissemination of technical progress. If the investment in one sector necessary to obtain a plant or a series of plants incorporating superior techniques exceeds the amount of surplus available for investment in that sector, or if it exceeds all the surplus available in the economy, not only will technical progress be biased, but in order for it to be realized, reduction of consumption (and of wages) will be required. This may well be impossible in the circumstances of the country seeking to introduce the innovation. In this case, a better decision would seem that of adopting non-superior techniques even though superior ones are present. The problem is a real one for small countries. Since technical research and technical progress primarily originate in countries with greater economic dimensions (however these are defined), superior techniques will reflect the greater availability of resources. Rates of investment will thus always have to be higher in the smaller than in the larger economies. An alternate solution would be for smaller economies to specialize, if possible, in the production and export of those commodities whose production methods are not influenced by size. The smaller economies may also be subject to periodical adjustment crises. Under these conditions, a movement toward integration among smaller economies is likely. There is no doubt that the tendencies described here exist among advanced as well as among underdeveloped economies. What influence these tendencies have on the capitalist development process and on the equilibrium of each economy we do not know.

THE COMPARISON BETWEEN DIFFERENT ECONOMIES

These observations cannot be made part of a generalized model. In the text it was pointed out that the rationalizing principle of each capitalist system resides in the goals of the entrepreneurial class. It does not seem possible, however, to compare two economies—even two capitalist economies—both because the problem of measuring values cannot be solved and because the measurement problem becomes very difficult to comprehend when the more restricted viewpoint of the economist is abandoned and economic systems are judged in their entirety, including the social and political instruments used by the entrepreneurial class to attain its ends.

Nonetheless, the classification of different economic systems remains feasible. Capitalism is not a closed system. In the past, the capitalist system of production expanded to a great many countries. If the complex of aims of the capitalist economy expands to other economies, the system of values becomes, in essence, common to all. Therefore, it should be possible to compare different economies on the basis of the degree to which they have attained the goals of capitalism. It should be possible, at least, to apply to more than one economy the observations on the structure and the development of capitalism presented in this essay.

UNDERDEVELOPED ECONOMIES

A permanent characteristic of the international capitalist system is the existence of advanced economies alongside backward economies. Many economists have repeatedly stated that the latter, although part of the capitalist universe, have all the characteristics of economies in a state of exploitation and have advanced as a proof the statistical observation that the secular trend of the terms of trade for backward economies is downward.[5] Since these countries present a very simple economic structure, usually based on the exports of a limited number of commodities to advanced economies, there should exist a connection between the exploitation and the capitalist system of production.

A number of interpretations of this relationship have been proposed. However, most of them seem to be too facile. Rosa Luxemburg, for example, advances the hypothesis that the exploitation of colonial economies on the part of industrialized countries is an attempt to permit an expansion of the accumulation process, while avoiding the otherwise necessary increase in real wages within the

[5] See R. Prebisch, "El desarollo economico de America Latina y algunos de sus principales problemas," *El trimestre economico* (July–September, 1949). C. P. Kindleberger links this tendency to the existence of monopolies; see his *The Terms of Trade: A European Case Study* (London, 1956), "I 'terms of trade' e lo sviluppo economico," *Studi economici* (January–February, 1957). The literature is abundant on this question and cuts across many areas of economics. For an abstract model, see H. G. Johnson, *International Trade and Economic Growth* (London, 1958), chap. iii, especially pp. 71 and 105.

industrialized economy.[6] One cannot deny that there may be a portion of truth in this hypothesis. But it does not seem a sufficient explanation, principally because the capitalist system has in effect increased real wages. I am not able to give a general interpretation of this phenomenon. There does exist, however, an observation which may clarify, at least in part, the nature of the relationship between the capitalist system and underdeveloped economies.

THE DIFFERENTIATION OF PROFIT RATES IN THE INTERNATIONAL ECONOMY

The principles on which the differentiation of profit rates within a capitalist economy is based (cf. Chapter 3 above) can be extended to an international system. Capitalism is based on the profit motive. If the differentiation of profit rates is limited to domestic economies, some domestic producers will have to be content with a lower rate of profit. A simple way to minimize the differences among classes of profits within an economy is to confine the production of commodities whose consumption increases least rapidly (and, in turn, of commodities which go to produce those commodities) to subordinated economies. The separation of the productive sectors can in this way be made more rigid, not so much for obvious geographical reasons, but because the subordinated economy is at a more primitive stage of capitalism and will be contented with a lower profit rate more easily. This may explain why many colonial countries concentrate on agricultural production. These countries, therefore, necessarily present a declining trend in their terms of trade, since they specialize in the production of commodities the consumption of which has a minimal income elasticity in the advanced importing countries. As a result, underdeveloped economies can do nothing to change the long-term trend in terms of trade unless they shift to producing commodities the consumption of which has a high income elasticity in the consuming countries and, therefore, a higher profit rate. A number of economists think that the capitalist system in advanced countries is capable of preventing the autonomous production of commodities of high income elasticity in underdeveloped countries.

[6] See her *Accumulation of Capital* (New York, 1965), chap. xxx; M. Kalecki (*Economic Dynamics*, pp. 53–54) advances the same opinion.

APPENDIX B

THE CHOICE OF TECHNIQUES

As a result of the procedure followed in the discussion of the problem of the technical conditions of production in Chapter 4 above, it is now possible to offer a new formulation of the problem of the "choice of techniques." This problem arose when, in a number of countries, a certain amount of investment planning was found necessary to stimulate a rate of economic growth adequate to the expectations of society. Plan policies are neither able nor (in most cases) intended to change, to any substantial degree, the structure of the capitalist market, since they take as *given*, certain "natural" trends of the economy; however, in a few important exceptions (e.g., India), the planning process does exercise a considerable influence on the private sector.

A complex and rewarding discussion on this subject has been taking place in recent years among economists.[1] The discussion has centered around the following question: in the absence of a market that can automatically establish a system of priorities (and thus of values), what are the fundamental principles on which an optimum choice of the techniques of production to be adopted in a planned economy should be based?

THE NEOCLASSICAL CRITERION

We are in a completely planned economy. Since the authorities control both the sector producing investment goods (K) and the sector producing consumer goods (C), choices made at the level of the individual enterprise will have a parallel effect at the level of the economy. Accumulation will always be adequate to maintain

---

[1] Only a few contributions will be mentioned: J. J. Polack, "Balance of Payments Problems of Countries Reconstructing with Help of Foreign Loans," *Quarterly Journal of Economics* (February, 1943); A. E. Kahn, "Investment Criteria in Development Programs," *ibid.* (February, 1951); H. B. Chenery, "The Application of Investment Criteria," *ibid.* (February, 1953); M. H. Dobb, "Second Thoughts on Capital Intensity," *Review of Economic Studies* (1956–57), pp. 33–42; F. M. Bator, "On Capital Productivity, Input Allocation and Growth," *Quarterly Journal of Economics* (February, 1957). A clear exposition of the question is given by A. K. Sen, *Choice of Techniques: An Aspect of the Theory of Planned Economic Development* (Oxford, 1960).

full employment, given the existence of a formal organ of direction. Let us suppose that this organ has perfect knowledge of the conditions existing in the economy (that it is "omniscient"): then there is no measurement problem, for the aims of the system are established by the central authority. Let us suppose also that the economic system under discussion is rigidly isolated and that full employment conditions prevail. To exemplify the problem of the choice of techniques as it has been discussed in recent literature, I have adapted Figure 4 from A. K. Sen.[2]

The positive ordinate axis (P_C) represents the total output of sector C, the negative ordinate axis (E_K) represents employment in

FIGURE 4

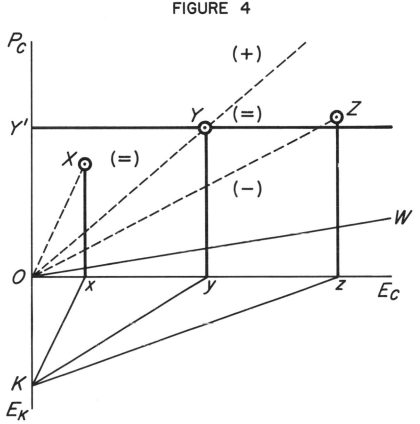

[2] "Some Notes on the Choice of Capital Intensity in Development Planning," *Quarterly Journal of Economics* (November, 1957); reproduced by permission of Harvard University Press.

sector K, and the abscissae axis (E_C), employment in sector C. The distance OK represents the amount of labor employable in sector K with C's present surplus of production over consumption. At any given moment of time, according to the neoclassical assumptions, there would exist various alternative production techniques. Let us suppose that there are three possible production techniques, no one superior to any other, X, Y, and Z, technique X having the greatest productivity (measured by the slope of OX) and the highest proportion of capital[3] (measured by the slope of Kx). If the wage rate is introduced—represented by W, or expressed in terms of commodities produced by sector C—a choice among the different techniques is possible. The technique that will furnish the maximum rate of investable surplus (measured by the distance between X, Y, and Z and OW) will clearly be preferable (in Fig. 4, technique Y will be the optimum one at the current level of wages). Let us turn to the figure again: the signs +, −, and = indicate the areas of the quadrant in which techniques are always superior, inferior, or open to a possible choice of the neoclassical type, respectively in relation to Y. According to neoclassical hypotheses, since inferior techniques will never be preferred and since superior techniques will be chosen *ipso facto*, the choice of techniques will be possible both in the area at the lower left of Y, indicated by =, in which the alternative techniques produce a greater output per man but yield a total output lower than does Y, and in the area at the upper right of Y, also indicated by =, in which alternative techniques show a lower output per man but yield a higher total output than does Y.

IS THERE A CHOICE OF TECHNIQUE?

As was observed in Chapter 4, the possibility that a choice of the neoclassical type may occur is not based on any empirical proof. On the contrary, for the reasons indicated there, there exists at least one other formulation of the problem which is logically stronger and certainly simpler, although it too lacks an empirical proof. Since at the beginning of the development process there exists only one technique, and since it is equally difficult technologically to invent a superior technique or a non-superior one, entrepreneurs (or planners) will always adopt superior techniques. A

---

[3] It is assumed that the period of production and the physical life span of plants do not change at the change of technology.

choice among techniques X, Y, and Z, as given in Figure 4, loses its meaning.

FIGURE 5

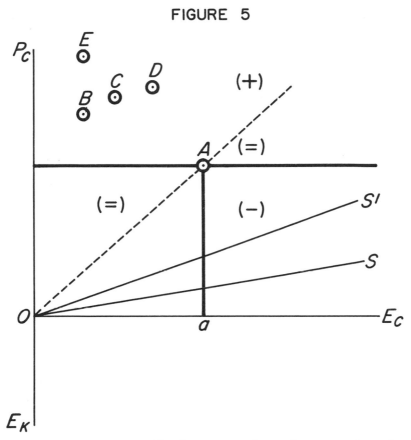

Figure 5 gives a possible illustration of our alternative formulation. Let us suppose that technique A, superior to a previously utilized technique, is the one prevalent in the economy at a given moment, and that for some reason—for example, because of an increase in wage rates, represented by a shift of OW—the investable surplus decreases. The planner will demand from his scientists a new superior technique. Let us suppose that scientists offer not one but many techniques, all superior to technique A. This assumption can be expressed in a different way by stating that the planner is capable of making a choice among many superior techniques before they have been obtained. However, the techniques to be demanded cannot be in a non-superiority relationship to each other. It would be absurd for the planner to set for himself the objective of choosing among possible alternative superior techniques (in relation to A) that are not also in a superiority relationship among themselves, since it is as difficult to invent superior as to invent non-superior techniques. In Figure 5, the planner will never try to make a choice among techniques which have a $B-C-D$ relationship because, given the argument of equal difficulty, he can always prefer, whatever the wage rate, technique E. There is clearly no reason to re-create, in this case, the neoclassical choice.

CHARACTER OF TECHNICAL PROGRESS AND CHOICE OF TECHNIQUES

It is conceivable, however, that the superior technique to be demanded may be neutral, capital-using, or capital-saving. If the planner is conscious of the influence that a biased technique has on the economy as a whole, he should be able to make a choice on a new technique. If he can make a choice in relation to the character of technical progress, he cannot but prefer neutral technical progress. Taking as a hypothesis that the planner, like the entrepreneurs in our model, does not "consume" and invests all "his" income, let us examine the two cases of biased technical progress and briefly analyze their effects on the economy.

When technical progress with a capital-using bias is introduced, *less* capital (investment) is freed than what is necessary to employ the amount of labor freed by the new technique. The rate of accumulation is then insufficient to maintain full employment, consumption and total sales will decrease as unemployment appears, and the economy will enter a crisis.[4] When technical progress having a capital-saving bias is introduced, *more* capital (investment) is freed than what is necessary to employ the amount of labor freed by the new techniques. The rate of accumulation is then in excess of full employment requirements, and the economy experiences inflation.

Both choices are clearly inferior to the choice of neutral techni-

---

[4] In dealing with a similar problem, Mrs. Robinson argues as though the rate of accumulation could be maintained, because entrepreneurs will somehow find the resources necessary for investment. It is not clear, however, where these resources come from, since the system is already working at full capacity.

cal progress. In any case, it does not seem likely that the planner is really in a position to make a decision of this kind. Innovations are introduced in a great many production lines, often at the same time. Since the distinction among the three characters of technical progress is based on the relative influence that technical progress has on sectors K or C, a choice is possible only insofar as these sectors are in practice distinguishable. It is more probable that the character of technical progress is given by the *scientists* to the *planner*. Even in this case, in all likelihood technical progress will tend to be distributed at random among the three characters and, in the long run, for a large number of innovations, will tend to be neutral.

In a different sense, the planner does have the capability to influence the character of the superior techniques introduced into the economy. As in a capitalist regime, a planning regime demonstrates a law of efficiency for which the faster the rate of investment in research, the greater the rate of technical progress. The planner should thus be able to influence the dynamics of the different production lines. This is not the place to go more deeply into this question. It does have importance for long-term planning, however, especially for those countries in which the development process is already advanced and in which the influence of the foreign sector is relatively small.

INDEX

Paolo Leon, *Structural Change and Growth in Capitalism: A Set of Hypotheses*
Designed by Gerard A. Valerio
Composed in Palatino by Monotype Composition Company, Inc.
Printed offset by Universal Lithographers, Inc., on 60 pound P & S RRR
Bound by Maple Press Company in Columbia Riverside RV-1098